INTRODUCTION TO THE
ORDER OF MASS:

A Pastoral Resource of the Bishops' Committee on the Liturgy

INTRODUCTION TO THE ORDER OF MASS:

A Pastoral Resource of the Bishops' Committee on the Liturgy

PASTORAL LITURGY SERIES • **ONE**

BISHOPS' COMMITTEE ON THE LITURGY
UNITED STATES CONFERENCE OF CATHOLIC BISHOPS
United States Conference of Catholic Bishops • Washington, DC

The document *Introduction to the Order of Mass: A Pastoral Resource of the Bishops' Committee on the Liturgy* was developed as a resource by the Bishops' Committee on the Liturgy of the United States Conference of Catholic Bishops (USCCB). It was reviewed by the committee chairman, Francis Cardinal George, and has been authorized for publication by the undersigned.

Msgr. William P. Fay
General Secretary, USCCB

First Printing, July 2003

ISBN 1-57455-544-8

TABLE OF CONTENTS

ABBREVIATIONS

AAS   *Acta Apostolicæ Sedis, Commentarium officiale*. Vatican City: Vatican Polyglot Press, 1909-.

BLS   United States Conference of Catholic Bishops. *Built of Living Stones: Art, Architecture, and Worship*. Washington, D.C.: United States Conference of Catholic Bishops, 2000.

CCC   *Catechism of the Catholic Church*. 2nd ed. Washington, D.C.: United States Conference of Catholic Bishops-Libreria Editrice Vaticana, 2000.

CIC   *Code of Canon Law*.

CP   Congregation for Divine Worship. Instruction *Calendaria particularia* (*On the Revision of Particular Calendars and of the Propers for Offices and Masses*) (June 24, 1970): AAS 62 (1970).

DD   Pope John Paul II. Apostolic letter *Dies Domini* (*On Keeping the Lord's Day Holy*). AAS 90 (1998). Retrieved from Vatican website at *www.vatican.va*.

DMC   Congregation for Divine Worship. *Directory for Masses with Children* (November 1, 1973). In *Masses with Children*. Liturgy Documentary Series 12. Washington, D.C.: United States Conference of Catholic Bishops, 1996.

EP   Congregation for Divine Worship. Circular letter *Eucharistiæ participationem* (*Circular Letter to the Presidents of the Conferences of Bishops on the Eucharistic Prayers*) (April 27, 1973): AAS 65 (1973). In *Vatican Council II: Vol. 1: The Conciliar and Post Conciliar Documents*, edited by Austin Flannery. Northport, N.Y.: Costello Publishing, 1996.

EPMC   Sacred Congregation for Divine Worship. Introduction to *Eucharistic Prayers for Masses with Children* (November 1, 1974). In *Masses with Children*. Liturgy Documentary Series 12. Washington, D.C.: United States Conference of Catholic Bishops, 1996.

EuchMyst   Congregation of Rites. Instruction *Eucharisticum mysterium* (*Instruction on the Worship of the Eucharistic Mystery*) (May 25, 1967): AAS 59 (1967). In *Vatican Council II: Vol. 1: The Conciliar and Post Conciliar Documents*, edited by Austin Flannery. Northport, N.Y.: Costello Publishing, 1996.

GILH   *General Instruction of the Liturgy of the Hours.*
        Liturgy Documentary Series 5. Washington,
        D.C.: United States Conference of Catholic
        Bishops, 2002.

GIRM   *General Instruction of the Roman Missal.* Liturgy
        Documentary Series 2. Washington, D.C.: United
        States Conference of Catholic Bishops, 2003.

GNLYC   Congregation of Rites. *General Norms for
        the Liturgical Year and the Calendar* (March
        21, 1969). Vatican City: Vatican Polyglot
        Press, 1969.

GS   Vatican Council II. *Gaudium et spes* (*Pastoral
        Constitution on the Church in the Modern
        World*) (December 7, 1965). In *Vatican
        Council II: The Basic Sixteen Documents,*
        edited by Austin Flannery. Northport, N.Y.:
        Costello Publishing, 1996.

IC   Congregation for the Discipline of the
        Sacraments. Instruction *Immensæ caritatis*
        (*Instruction on Facilitating Sacramental Eucharistic
        Communion in Particular Circumstances*) (January
        29, 1973): AAS 65 (1973). In *Vatican Council II:
        Vol. 1: The Conciliar and Post Conciliar
        Documents,* edited by Austin Flannery.
        Northport, N.Y.: Costello Publishing, 1996.

ID   Sacred Congregation for the Sacraments and
            Divine Worship. Instruction *Inaestimabile donum*
            (*Norms for the Worship of the Eucharistic
            Mystery*) (April 3, 1980): AAS 72 (1980).

LG   Vatican Council II. *Lumen gentium* (*Dogmatic
            Constitution on the Church*) (November 21,
            1964). In *Vatican Council II: The Basic Sixteen
            Documents*, edited by Austin Flannery.
            Northport, N.Y.: Costello Publishing, 1996.

LM   *Lectionary for Mass, Second Typical Edition:
            Introduction* (1981). Liturgy Documentary
            Series 1. Washington, D.C.: United States
            Conference of Catholic Bishops, 1998.

MusSacr   Congregation of Rites. Instruction *Musicam
            sacram* (*Instruction on Music in the Liturgy*)
            (March 5, 1967): AAS 59 (1967). In *Vatican
            Council II: Vol. 1: The Conciliar and Post
            Conciliar Documents*, edited by Austin Flannery.
            Northport, N.Y.: Costello Publishing, 1996.

RCIA   *Rite of Christian Initiation of Adults* (2nd English
            translation, 1985). Washington, D.C.: United
            States Conference of Catholic Bishops, 1988.

SC   Vatican Council II. *Sacrosanctum Concilium*
            (*Constitution on the Sacred Liturgy*) (December
            4, 1963). In *Vatican Council II: The Basic Sixteen
            Documents*, edited by Austin Flannery.
            Northport, N.Y.: Costello Publishing, 1996.

INTRODUCTION

The *Pastoral Introduction to the Order of Mass* was approved in 1997 by the National Conference of Catholic Bishops (later the United States Conference of Catholic Bishops [USCCB]) and was revised in 2000 by the Congregation for Divine Worship and the Discipline of the Sacraments in the light of changes introduced to the *Order of Mass* in the *Institutio Generalis Missalis Romani*. In the letter accompanying the Congregation's revision, Cardinal Jorge Medina Estévez, then-Prefect, described the *Pastoral Introduction* as a "useful pastoral instrument for liturgical formation of the People of God" that addresses "appropriately and felicitously the specific ecclesial and pastoral context of the Conference's territory."

At its June 2002 meeting, the USCCB Committee on the Liturgy reviewed the emended text of the *Pastoral Introduction*, incorporated into it the recently approved and confirmed U.S. adaptations to the *General Instruction of the Roman Missal*, and mandated its publication.

The *Pastoral Introduction to the Order of Mass* is not a legislative document. Juridical authority in the matters dealt with in this resource is found in the *Missale Romanum* itself and in the adaptations that appear in the U.S. edition of the *General Instruction of the Roman Missal* (2003). The *Roman Missal*, including the rubrics found in the *Order of Mass* and the *General Instruction*, is the authentic source for what the Church requires in the celebration of the Sacred Liturgy.

This *Pastoral Introduction to the Order of Mass* is designed to assist in the training of various liturgical ministers, as well as the popular formation of the whole People of God in preparing all to receive the new *Roman Missal*. This resource is intended to be, in the words of the Prefect of the Congregation for Divine Worship, "a useful pastoral instrument for liturgical formation of the People of God."

The goal of all liturgical formation is described by the *Roman Missal* itself:

> In the celebration of Mass the faithful form a holy people, a people whom God has made his own, a royal priesthood, so that they may give thanks to God and offer the spotless Victim not only through the hands of the priest but also together with him, and so that they may learn to offer themselves. They should, moreover, endeavor to make this clear by their deep religious sense and their charity toward brothers and sisters who participate with them in the same celebration.
>
> Thus, they are to shun any appearance of individualism or division, keeping before their eyes that they have only one Father in heaven and accordingly are all brothers and sisters to each other.[1]

---

1   GIRM, no. 95.

Such a vision often challenges the rugged individualism of Americans. Yet any desire to imprint the identity of a particular community upon the liturgy must be tempered by the firm conviction that the Mysteries of our redemption transcend individuals and communities who celebrate the Sacred Liturgy. True participation in the Mass presumes a willingness to die to self. True participation in the Mass requires radical obedience to Christ and to his Church: a willingness to die and rise with him, which is the very stuff of the Eucharistic Sacrifice and Banquet.

The formation of the People of God and the ministers of the altar must, therefore, be unlike any other educational endeavor. Liturgical formation "must above all be spiritual,"[2] though a familiarity with the rites and patterns of the prayer of the Mass is essential. Good liturgy is the product not so much of a well-known rubric as much as a well-trained heart. While the rites and prayers that the Church gives us make up a treasury of the Church's understanding of her Lord and what he asks of her, they are primarily the means to a full, conscious, and active participation in the Paschal Mystery through which Christ redeems his Beloved and joins her to himself in glory.

---

2   LM, no. 55.

May this resource be a help to God's holy people as they seek to join their voices with the angels in one grand chorus of joyous praise. Thus, may the sacred mysteries we celebrate here on earth prepare us for and portend that for which we long and he for whom we wait. "Blessed are those who are called to the supper of the Lamb!"

Msgr. James P. Moroney
Executive Director
USCCB Secretariat for the Liturgy

I.

THE CELEBRATION
OF MASS

1. For every celebration of the Eucharist, a portion of the People of God is summoned to assemble under the authority of the diocesan Bishop, or of a Bishop or priest delegated by him, as part of the body of Christ and thus to fulfill the Lord's command to "do this in memory of me" (Lk 22:19). In this most sacred action of Christ and the Church, the memorial of his death and resurrection is celebrated; God is adored in spirit and in truth; the Church identifies herself with the saving sacrifice that her Lord perpetuates and, nourished by his Body and Blood, looks forward in joyful hope to sharing in the supper of the Lamb in the heavenly kingdom.[3]

2. At the Last Supper the Lord spoke to his disciples, took bread and wine, gave thanks, broke the bread, and gave them the bread of life and the cup of eternal salvation. After his resurrection from the dead, two disciples recognized his presence in these same actions: speaking, taking bread, giving thanks, breaking, and sharing (see Lk 24:13-35). In the Eucharist, the Church to this day makes Christ's memorial and celebrates his presence in the same sequence of actions: in the Liturgy of the Word, the Church listens with heart burning as the Lord speaks

---

3   See EuchMyst, no. 3a-c.

to her again, and she responds with words of praise and petition; in the Liturgy of the Eucharist, the Church takes bread and wine, gives thanks, breaks the bread, and receives the Body and Blood of Christ.[4]

3. These two principal parts of the Mass are so closely connected as to form one single act of worship: the table of God's word and of Christ's Body and Blood is prepared, and from it the faithful are instructed and nourished. The spoken word of God announces the history of salvation; the Eucharist embodies it in the sacramental signs of the liturgy. In addition to these two parts, the introductory rites prepare the people for word and Eucharist, and the concluding rite brings the people's worship to a close and sends them out to witness and serve.[5]

4. The celebration of Mass is the action of Christ and the People of God—ministers and congregation. Within the one body of Christ are many gifts and responsibilities. But just as each organ and limb is necessary for the sound functioning of the body (see 1 Cor 12), so every member of the liturgical assembly gathered by Christ has a part to play in the action of the whole. It is, therefore, of the greatest importance that in all

---

4   See GIRM, no. 72.
5   See GIRM, no. 28; see LM, no. 10.

circumstances and on every occasion the celebration be organized so that priest, deacon, lay ministers, and faithful may all take their own parts. The participation of all is demanded by the nature of the liturgy and, for the faithful, is their right and duty by reason of their Baptism.[6]

By apostolic tradition, the Church gathers on the Lord's Day, the Church's primordial feast day, to celebrate the Lord's Supper. This Sunday Eucharist, which gathers the local community and in which all play their proper parts, is the primary manifestation of the parish community and thus deserves particularly diligent consideration and preparation.[7] The celebration of other sacraments, when the Roman Ritual allows, may be accommodated within it.

In the celebration of the Eucharist, all who are present participate according to their role and function in the Liturgy.[8] A celebration is the work of the whole body of Christ; the ministers and other members of the congregation have a part in the action and have a contribution to make. Each of these special services is performed for the good of the whole and for the glory of God.

---

6   See SC, nos. 14, 28; see also GIRM, nos. 16, 17, 18, 20.
7   See SC, nos. 49, 106; see GNLYC, no. 4.
8   See SC, no. 28.

LITURGICAL MINISTERS AND THE GATHERED ASSEMBLY

5. All present contribute to the Eucharistic celebration by their full, active, and conscious participation and, where necessary or appropriate, by the carrying out of the responsibilities of their particular order or function. By doing all and only those parts that belong to them, ordained and lay ministers and all members of the congregation contribute to the participation of all and show the Church as the Body of Christ, actively engaged in worship of the living God with the help of various orders and ministries.[9]

6. The composition of the Eucharistic assembly ideally represents and reflects the nature of the Church herself, which is hierarchically ordered.[10] The very arrangement of the celebration in its various ministries shows that all the baptized have a place in the Church—women and men, young and old, people of every race and tongue. Through the active participation of the faithful and the variety of liturgical ministries in the Church, the Body of Christ is built up.

7. All who exercise a role within the liturgical assembly need proper preparation for their responsibilities. They are to have the competence to perform the particular role entrusted to them.

---

9   See GIRM, no. 91.
10   See GIRM, no. 16.

8. The formation of those who exercise a liturgical ministry is both spiritual and technical. Although this formation varies in extent and depth depending upon the nature of the particular role, it normally has liturgical, biblical, and technical components. Through liturgical formation they acquire an understanding of the Mass as a whole, with particular emphasis on the parts of the Mass for which they have specific responsibility. Through biblical formation they are helped to understand the cycle of Scripture readings and to perceive the revealed message of the Scriptures through the light of faith. They also learn the intimate connection between the two principal parts of the Mass: the Liturgy of the Word and the Liturgy of the Eucharist. Through training in the particular skills of their ministry, they learn to make the best use of their personal gifts and strengths in order to communicate the person and message of Christ by the reverent use of word, gesture, and movement.

9. Opportunities should be made available periodically for liturgical ministers to pray together and to receive continuing formation for their tasks. These occasions may provide for their ongoing training and for the improvement of their abilities to facilitate the liturgical celebration.

10. The words and actions of the Liturgy give verbal and physical expression to the profound realities of God's gracious activity and the Church's attitude in response to God. The liturgical ministers are, therefore, to give care to the verbal and physical elements of the Liturgy.

- When speaking or singing, liturgical ministers use a strong, clear voice and strive for a measured delivery.

- By reverent posture, gesture, and movement, they reinforce the words of the liturgy and help to facilitate the response of the faithful.

- When not performing particular duties, they join with the rest of the congregation in their actions and responses. At these times they listen, respond, and sing with all present and so continue to contribute to the worship of the whole body.

Priest Celebrant

11. In the celebration of the Eucharist, Christ is present in the person of the presiding priest. Every celebration of the Eucharist is presided over in the person of Christ by the Bishop or a priest. The Bishop or priest leads the people in praying, in listening and responding to God's word, and in offering the sacrifice through Christ in the Spirit to the Father. He proclaims the message of salvation in preaching the homily and ministers the bread and cup of salvation.[11]

12. By virtue of the sacrament of Holy Orders, as well as by the depth of the priest's prayerfulness and the dignity and humility of his bearing, the people should be able to recognize the living

---

11   See GIRM, nos. 27, 92, 93.

presence of Christ, who spoke as one with authority yet as one who came not to be served but to serve. Likewise, the priest is conscious that he presides in the name of Christ over a community that Christ has gathered in his own name.[12]

- Through his liturgical presidency, the priest celebrant encourages the participation of others and coordinates them into one harmonious action. Rather than appropriating the functions of others, he is responsible for seeing that everything is done well.[13]

- The priest exercises his responsibility chiefly in the praying of the presidential prayers: the Opening Prayer, the Prayer Over the Offerings, the Prayer After Communion, and, supremely, the Eucharistic Prayer. Presiding in the person of Christ, he addresses these prayers to God not only in his own name, but in that of the gathered assembly and of the entire People of God.[14]

- In some circumstances, the priest may also facilitate the conscious participation of the congregation by brief and helpful comments and introductions: for example, at the beginning of the celebration, before the readings and the Eucharistic Prayer, or at the dismissal.[15]

---

12   See GIRM, no. 93.
13   See LM, no. 38; see EP, no. 17.
14   See GIRM, no. 30.
15   See GIRM, no. 31; see LM, no. 42.

- The appropriateness of the celebrant's eye contact with the congregation during the celebration depends on what particular part of the liturgical action is transpiring. Maintaining eye contact is appropriate when the priest addresses the people, but not when he is addressing God in prayer.

- The readings are usually proclaimed by other ministers, but the homily is reserved to the Bishop, priest, or deacon and is ordinarily given by the Bishop or priest presiding (see nos. 92-94). The homily is an integral part of the Liturgy, particularly when the community gathers for its Sunday celebration of the Eucharist.[16]

- Other priests are encouraged to participate in the celebration of the Eucharist by means of concelebration. The distinctive rites laid down for concelebration of the Eucharist are intended to signify the unity of the priesthood, of the sacrifice, and of the whole People of God. In the absence of a deacon, some aspects of his role are carried out by some of the priest concelebrants.[17]

Deacon

13. The deacon, whose order has been held in high honor since the early Church, holds, after the priest, the "first place among those who minister in the celebration of the Eucharist."[18]

---

16   See GIRM, no. 66.
17   See GIRM, nos. 114, 199, 208; see "USCCB Guidelines for the Concelebration of the Eucharist" (GCE), *BCL Newsletter* (November 1999): 98-105.
18   GIRM, no. 94.

In communion with the Bishop and the priests, the deacon's service for the People of God is the *diakonia* of liturgy, word, and charity.[19]

- The deacon proclaims the Gospel reading. On occasion, he may be invited to deliver the homily, and he also ordinarily announces the intentions at the General Intercessions or Prayers of the Faithful.[20] If the *Book of the Gospels* is used, the deacon may carry it before the presiding priest in the entrance procession. He omits the sign of reverence, places the book on the altar, and then, with the priest, kisses the altar.[21]

- In the Liturgy of the Eucharist, the deacon helps to distribute Holy Communion to the people, especially as minister of the chalice. In this connection, he also prepares the table and gifts, elevates the chalice at the doxology, and may assist with the breaking of the bread and the preparation of the chalice or chalices at Communion.

- As the servant of the entire gathered assembly and its worship, the deacon assists the priest at the chair and at the altar. He is also called to give certain directions and invitations to the congregation, especially regarding

19   See GIRM, no. 94; see LG, no. 29; see Roman Pontifical, *Rite of Ordination of a Bishop, of Priests, and of Deacons, editio typica altera* (2003), no. 199.
20   See GIRM, nos. 71, 911; see LM, no. 50.
21   See GIRM, no. 173.

movement or posture.[22] When incense is used, the deacon helps with its preparation and, where indicated, may incense the priest, the people, and the *Book of the Gospels*.

Lector

14. In proclaiming the word of God, lectors exercise their responsibility in the liturgical celebration. God speaks to the faithful through them, and the effectiveness of their proclamation of God's word depends significantly on their conviction, preparation, and delivery.

15. The richness in the quantity and variety of readings in the Lectionary challenges those who are called upon to proclaim the Scriptures at Mass. The individual sacred authors reflected on the meaning of God's action in history from their own perspectives and in their own styles. They employed various literary forms to convey the message of salvation: ranging, for example, from narratives and the poetry of the psalms to prophetic oracles and parables, from theological expositions to apocalyptic visions. An awareness of the literary form of a particular reading or psalm and a knowledge of the sacred author's style enables the lector or psalmist to proclaim more fully and with greater understanding the tone and content of the text.

• The liturgical assembly needs lectors. Proper measures must therefore be taken to ensure that qualified persons

---

22   See GIRM, no. 94.

have been trained to carry out this ministry. Whenever more than one reading is to be proclaimed, it is better to have a different lector for each reading.[23]

- The Responsorial Psalm is led by a psalmist or cantor; but, if necessary, it may be led by a lector.[24] In this case, it is preferable that it be led by someone other than the reader of the first reading, in order to respect the force and effectiveness of the Liturgy of the Word as proclamation and response.

- When no deacon is present, a lector may carry the *Book of the Gospels* before the presiding priest in the entrance procession and lay it on the altar. If the *Book of the Gospels* is carried in procession by either the deacon or a lector, the Lectionary is prepared on the ambo beforehand. The Lectionary is never carried in procession.[25]

- All readings are proclaimed from the ambo.[26]

Gathered Assembly

16. Christ is always present in the Church, particularly in her liturgical celebrations. In the celebration of Mass, which is a memorial of the sacrifice of the Cross, Christ is truly present in

---

23 See GIRM, no. 109; see LM, no. 52.
24 See GIRM, no. 196; see LM, no. 22.
25 See GIRM, nos. 118b, 120d, 194-195.
26 See GIRM, nos. 58, 309.

the assembly he gathers to himself: "Where two or three come together in my name, there am I in their midst" (Mt 18:20).[27] At Mass, the faithful form

> a holy people, a people whom God has made his own, a royal priesthood, so that they may give thanks to God and offer the spotless Victim not only through the hands of the priest but also together with him, and so that they may learn to offer themselves. They should, moreover, endeavor to make this clear by their deep religious sense and their charity toward brothers and sisters who participate with them in the same celebration.[28]

17. The liturgical assembly is not a random group of individuals but is, rather, the gathering of God's people to exercise its royal priesthood in the sacrifice of praise. Its structure and ordering are a reflection of the Church herself, governed and served by the Bishop, priests, and deacons. The celebration is organized to encourage and foster an awareness of the liturgical assembly's common dependence on God and each other as well as its common dignity and purpose.

- The dialogues between the priest—or, where appropriate, the deacon—and the congregation and the acclamations have special value as signs of communal action and as means of effective communication.[29]

---

27   See SC, no. 7; see GIRM, no. 27.
28   GIRM, no. 95.
29   See GIRM, no. 34.

- Singing is an important expression of communal awareness and purpose.

- Uniformity in posture and gesture likewise expresses and fosters a unity of spirit and purpose.

- Accommodation should be made where possible to facilitate the participation of persons with special needs.

- Care should be taken to recognize the needs of children who may be a part of the assembly. In particular cases where the greater part of those participating are preadolescent children, the adaptations provided in the *Directory for Masses with Children* may be used.[30]

Liturgical Musicians

18. A psalmist, a cantor, an organist, other instrumentalists, a choir, and a director of music aid the gathered assembly's full participation in singing responses, acclamations, and other texts set to music. These musicians exercise a genuine liturgical function and, by their role, help to add beauty and solemnity to the celebration.[31]

- The psalmist has the special task of drawing all present into the proclamation of the word of God in the psalm by

---

30   See DMC, nos. 16-19.
31   See GIRM, nos. 103-104.

introducing the psalm responses and Alleluia or Gospel Acclamation and by singing the verses of the Responsorial Psalm and the Alleluia and Gospel verses.[32] The psalmist may also introduce all antiphons and sing the verses of the psalms used. The role of the psalmist and cantor may be carried out by the same person.

- The cantor's function is to lead and encourage the congregation in singing. In preparation for the liturgical celebration, the cantor may introduce and teach new music to the people.[33]

- The organ and other instruments not only support and encourage participation through song but also, in their own right, can powerfully assist contemplation and express praise and a variety of human feelings before God. The choir remains at all times a part of the gathered assembly. It can serve that assembly by leading it in sung prayer and by reinforcing or enhancing its singing—for example, by sharing the singing of verses or sections of a hymn or song; alternately, by introducing a sung response or antiphon; or through harmonizing or elaborating in other ways. Occasionally, the choir may appropriately sing alone more elaborate music—for example, an anthem—that can aid the prayerful reflection of the congregation.

---

32   See GIRM, no. 102.
33   See GIRM, no. 104.

- Even at celebrations when no choir sings, basic musical participation can be ensured by an instrumentalist and one or more cantors, or by a cantor alone. Especially through responsorial singing, they can draw the people into singing together.[34]

Extraordinary Ministers of Holy Communion

19. "Since the Eucharistic Celebration is the Paschal Banquet, it is desirable that in keeping with the Lord's command, his Body and Blood should be received as spiritual food by the faithful who are properly disposed."[35] If a particularly large number are to receive Holy Communion, the priest celebrant may need assistance in distributing Holy Communion, so that the rite is not unduly long.[36]

20. Bishops, priests, and deacons are the ordinary ministers of Holy Communion. Instituted acolytes, when available, may assist as extraordinary ministers. Occasionally, however, this assistance will be given by other extraordinary ministers of Holy Communion, either formally commissioned for a given period or, in case of necessity, deputed as needed by the priest celebrant.

21. These ministers serve Christ present in the gathered assembly by ministering his Body and Blood to their brothers and sisters. They also serve the unity of the worshiping community by

---

34   See GIRM, no. 104.
35   GIRM, no. 80.
36   See IC, section 1, no. 1c; see GIRM, no. 281.

taking Holy Communion to those members who are prevented by sickness, old age, or other cause from taking part in the congregation. In accord with an ancient tradition, it is appropriate for Holy Communion to be taken directly from the Sunday Mass to the sick and to those unable to leave their homes.

- Those carrying out the various liturgical roles need not be accommodated in the sanctuary for the whole celebration. The extraordinary ministers of Holy Communion come forward from their place among the people after the reception of Holy Communion by the priest celebrant.

- After the Communion of the priest, the extraordinary ministers receive Communion from him. Then they receive the Sacred Vessels with the Body or Blood of the Lord for distribution to the faithful. Extraordinary ministers of Holy Communion never receive Holy Communion in the manner of concelebrants.

- The deacon or concelebrating priests assist in the preparation of the Eucharistic bread and chalices for Holy Communion. If it is necessary to use the hosts consecrated from a previous Mass, a priest or deacon should bring the reserved sacrament to the altar from the tabernacle, reverently but without ceremony.

- When the distribution of Holy Communion is complete, the deacon and the concelebrating priests—or, in their absence, the acolytes or other extraordinary ministers of Holy Communion—should return the Sacred Vessels to the altar, where the priests or deacons gather into one or more ciboria any remaining Sacred Hosts and then place them in the tabernacle. The Sacred Vessels are then brought to the altar or a side table. When more of the Precious Blood remains than was necessary for Communion, and if it is not consumed by the Bishop or priest celebrant, the deacon immediately and reverently consumes at the altar all of the Blood of Christ that remains; he may be assisted, if needed, by other deacons and priests. When extraordinary ministers of Holy Communion are present, they may consume what remains of the Precious Blood from their chalice of distribution. The Sacred Vessels should be purified by a priest, deacon, or instituted acolyte immediately or be left to be purified as soon as Mass has been completed.[37] The faculty may be given by the diocesan Bishop to the priest celebrant to be assisted, when necessary, even by extraordinary ministers of Holy Communion in the cleansing of the vessels after the distribution of Communion.

- When Holy Communion is being taken from Mass to the sick or those unable to leave their homes, the priest gives the pyx containing the Holy Eucharist to the deacons, acolytes, or extraordinary ministers of Holy Communion immediately after Communion has been distributed.

---

37   See GIRM, no. 182.

Alternatively, they may depart immediately after receiving Communion themselves, or even as part of the concluding procession of ministers.

Servers

22. In addition to the service of instituted acolytes, assistance at the altar by servers represents a long liturgical tradition. These servers enhance the quality of celebration for the whole gathered assembly by taking part in processions and by ensuring that all items required for the celebration are available at the appropriate moments.[38]

- Servers hold the book while the presiding priest proclaims the presidential prayers with outstretched hands. They bring and hold such things as the book, censer, water pitcher and towel, patens and ciboria, and microphones. They lead the entrance and concluding processions with the cross and candles. Carrying candles and, in more solemn celebrations, the censer, they escort the deacon (or priest) to the ambo and stand at his side while he proclaims the Gospel reading. On more solemn occasions, again bearing candles, they may accompany the procession with the gifts. They tend the censer and prepare it for the priest or deacon, and in the absence of a deacon they incense the priest and the congregation.

---

38   See GIRM, no. 100.

- The number of servers depends upon the circumstances and the tasks to be performed. More solemn celebrations should especially have a master of ceremonies with responsibility for ensuring that these various tasks are properly assigned and carried out.[39]

Ushers

23. St. Paul instructed the assembled community to "welcome one another as Christ has welcomed you, to the glory of God" (Rom 15:7). It will normally be appropriate for those commonly referred to as "ushers" to exercise their role by welcoming people at the door, providing them with all necessary books and aids, and helping them find their places.[40] The people are coming as invited guests of the Lord himself, to share in his supper as sisters and brothers. They will appreciate this more readily if they are made welcome by representatives of the community and acknowledged informally by their neighbors.

- In small and stable communities, a formal arrangement for welcoming may not be needed. But in larger assemblies with a more shifting attendance, special arrangements may be necessary so that visitors and those unfamiliar with the community and its worship may be put at ease and drawn into the celebration.

---

39   See GIRM, no. 106.
40   See GIRM, no. 105c-d.

- Ushers also help when members of the congregation become ill or otherwise need assistance.

- Ushers may assist with the collection of money and other gifts and with processions.

THE EUCHARISTIC CELEBRATION AND ITS SYMBOLS

24. "In the Liturgy the sanctification of women and men is given expression in symbols perceptible by the senses and is carried out in ways appropriate to each of them."[41] Taking bread and wine, pronouncing over these elements the words of Christ, and then breaking the bread and giving these Eucharistic elements to the faithful all constitute the principal symbolism of the Sacred Liturgy. The importance of this symbolism is further emphasized and conveyed by the entire ritual complex of words and actions set forth in the liturgical books authoritatively promulgated by the Church. Consequently, it is important that these actions be carried out in a correct and dignified manner so that they will truly be seen as actions of the Church herself in conformity with the will of Christ. Words clearly proclaimed, actions deliberately and gracefully performed, and elements and objects authentically made and reverently handled contribute to the integrity of the liturgy and allow its symbolism to work to greater effect.

---

41   SC, no. 7.

25. Bread and wine, breaking and sharing, eating and drinking, standing, kneeling, bowing, and greeting should not need to be explained. It is in sharing and experiencing them in their natural integrity and consistency that their spiritual significance and effect are appropriated.

Gesture and Posture

26. The active participation of the faithful is first of all interior, in that they inwardly participate in that which they outwardly hear, do, and say during the Liturgy. It is also exterior in that through their outward bearing and gestures they express their inner participation in the Liturgy. This ritual interplay between these elements points to the transcendence and the immanence of the living God.[42]

27. Since worship engages Christians fully, in every aspect of their being, they worship God with their bodies and feelings as well as their minds and spirits, with their hands and feet as well as their eyes and ears. The non-verbal elements of the Liturgy can express what cannot be articulated in words and, at times, can reinforce the spoken word. Because of their importance, the gestures and postures of the Liturgy are to be given the attention they require.

28. The people are called as members of an organic whole, not as disparate individuals. A Christian assembly that worships "with one heart and soul" (Acts 4:32) naturally moves toward and

---

42   See MusSacr, no. 15.

consciously chooses a common posture as a sign of its unity. Such common posture "both expresses and fosters the intention and spiritual attitude of the participants."[43]

Actions that the whole congregation performs together express its unity and cohesion in the Body of Christ. Such actions and gestures include, for example, making the Sign of the Cross, standing to pray, sitting to listen, kneeling in adoration, bowing to show reverence, striking the breast in sorrow for past personal sins, moving forward to present and receive, and exchanging the sign of peace.

Other actions are performed by the priest celebrant—for example, praying with hands raised and outstretched, blessing with hands extended over the people, showing the consecrated elements before the people, and breaking the Eucharistic bread (see nos. 130-131)—or by other ministers: for example, carrying the *Book of the Gospels*, incensing the people, and bowing to the altar.

POSTURE

29. Most English-speaking cultures share a common understanding of the significance of the postures of standing, sitting, and kneeling. One rises to greet people, to honor someone important, or to express readiness for action, or when seized with excitement. In Christian liturgical tradition, standing is the basic posture of an Easter people lifted up to greet their

---

43   GIRM, no. 42.

risen Lord. The congregation stands at Mass, for example, during the proclamation of the Gospel reading.[44]

30. One sits to listen, to rest, to watch. At Mass, for example, sitting is appropriate during the readings before the Gospel, during the homily, and at the Preparation of the Gifts.[45]

31. One kneels as a human gesture of submission. In Christian tradition, kneeling is an acknowledgment of one's creatureliness before God. It can signify penitence for sin, humility, reverence, and adoration.

- The United States Conference of Catholic Bishops (USCCB) may adapt the actions and postures described in the *Order of Mass*, in accord with local sensibilities and the meaning and character of the rite. The *recognitio* of the Holy See is required for such adaptations to take effect.[46]

- Accordingly, the USCCB has decided that, in general, the directives of the *Roman Missal* should be left unchanged but that paragraph no. 43 of the *General Instruction of the Roman Missal* should be adapted so that the people sit for the readings before the Gospel reading, for the Responsorial Psalm, and for the homily and the Preparation of the Gifts; and they may sit or kneel during the period of religious silence

---

44   See GIRM, no. 43.

45   See GIRM, no. 43.

46   See GIRM, nos. 43, 390.

after Communion, if doing so seems helpful. They should kneel beginning after the singing or recitation of the *Sanctus* (or "Holy, Holy") until after the Amen of the Eucharistic Prayer, except when prevented on occasion because of health, lack of space, the large number of people, or some other good reason. Those who do not kneel ought to make a profound bow when the priest genuflects after the consecration. The faithful kneel after the *Agnus Dei* (or "Lamb of God") unless the diocesan Bishop determines otherwise.

OTHER POSTURES AND GESTURES

32. Other gestures employed in the celebration of the Mass include bowing, kissing, genuflecting, and striking the breast. Each of these gestures has had a natural significance in human experience and in Christian liturgical tradition, but this significance may vary considerably according to culture and epoch. Bowing may be seen as a natural and gracious sign of respect— for instance, when passing the altar. Kissing is a more intense sign of reverence and respect. Genuflecting—an ancient gesture of fealty, reverence, and adoration—is now generally reserved for the veneration of Christ present in the Most Blessed Sacrament. Striking the breast is a sign of humility and self-abasement.

Words

33. Because the celebration of Mass is a communal activity, the priest celebrant and all others who have special parts to play need to give careful thought to the different kinds of verbal

communication with the congregation. Their manner of delivery should correspond to the nature or genre of the text, the scale and acoustics of the building, the form of the celebration, and the genius of the language.[47]

SACRED SCRIPTURE

34. Of exceptional importance among the texts of the Mass are the biblical readings (see nos. 84-86) with their accompanying scriptural chants. For even now, from the word of God handed down in writing, God speaks to the people: "and it is from the continued use of Sacred Scripture that the people of God, docile to the Holy Spirit under the light of faith, is enabled to bear witness to Christ before the world by its manner of life."[48]

PRESIDENTIAL PRAYERS

35. Among the texts assigned to the priest, the Eucharistic Prayer is of first importance as the high point of the whole celebration (see nos. 111-124). Next are the other presidential prayers: the Collect, the Prayer Over the Offerings, and the Prayer After Communion.

- These prayers are proclaimed by the priest alone, presiding in the person of Christ. They are addressed to God in the name of the entire People of God and of all who are present.[49]

---

47   See EP, no. 17; see GIRM, no. 38.
48   LM, no. 12.
49   See GIRM, no. 30.

- When the congregation is drawn into the prayer by the invitation "Let us pray," all observe some moment of silence in which they place themselves in God's presence and make their personal petitions.

- By a most ancient tradition of the Roman Rite, presidential prayers have a Trinitarian character, being addressed to God the Father (*Pater, Deus, Domine*) with and through the Son as mediator, in the unity and power of the Holy Spirit, who maintains the Church in communion and helps her to pray.

- The congregation makes the prayer its own and expresses its assent in the acclamation "Amen."

COMMON PRAYERS AND OTHER TEXTS

36. The dialogues between the priest and the congregation, as well as the acclamations, are particularly important as expressions of the prayer of the whole liturgical assembly. They are necessary as the very minimum form of communal participation, whatever the form of Mass. Some texts belong to all present and thus are recited or sung, as appropriate, by the priest and congregation together: for example, the acclamations, the Profession of Faith (or Creed), and the Lord's Prayer.[50]

---

50   See GIRM, nos. 34-37.

SUNG TEXTS

37. Various forms of prayer, by their very nature or because of their function in the Liturgy, lend themselves to being sung.

- The psalms used in the Liturgy—for example, the Responsorial Psalm and others designated in the *Roman Gradual* or *Simple Gradual*—are hymns and poems of praise intended for singing. The opening and communion antiphons, when used, likewise are texts that by their very nature should be sung, along with appropriate psalm verses.

- Other texts—for example, the acclamations—call all present to take them up and voice them in song with enthusiasm.

- On Sundays, solemnities, feasts, or more solemn occasions, elements of the Liturgy like the Eucharistic Prayer or at least its preface may be sung, as may the other presidential prayers. Since the Eucharistic Prayer is the central prayer and high point of the Mass, the singing of this prayer expresses the solemn nature of the day or occasion being celebrated.

INVITATIONS AND INTRODUCTIONS

38. At certain moments in the Mass, indicated in the rubrics, the deacon or presiding priest gives formal invitations to elicit the people's action, response, or silent preparation for prayer.

In addition, the presiding priest may facilitate the people's participation by brief and well-prepared comments.[51]

- All such introductions may be adapted to the different circumstances and occasions.

- The introductions or invitations may be expressed in the words provided or in similar words when this is foreseen by the rubrics.

PRIVATE PRAYERS

39. Some prayers prescribed in the Mass are personal prayers of the priest or deacon. These are by nature private and are recited inaudibly.[52] This also allows the faithful to pray silently in their own way during these moments.

Liturgical Music

40. As an art placed at the service of communal prayer, liturgical music is part of the liturgical action, one that is "a particularly apt way to express a joyful heart, accentuating the solemnity of the celebration and fostering the sense of a common faith and a shared love."[53] The inestimable treasure of liturgical music is considered integral to worship because it is so closely bound to the liturgical texts. The liturgical texts themselves—whether those taken from Sacred Scripture or those composed by the Church—are not to be altered in being set to music,

---

51   See GIRM, no. 31; see EP, no. 14.
52   See GIRM, no. 33.
53   DD, no. 50.

except insofar as this may be foreseen in the duly approved editions of the liturgical books themselves.[54] Keeping in mind the important place of signing in celebration, as a necessary and integral part of the liturgy, all musical settings of the text for the people's responses and acclamations in the *Order of Mass* and for special rites that occur in the course of the liturgical year must be submitted to the USCCB Secretariat for the Liturgy for review and approval before publication.

41. In all the arts, the Church has admitted styles from every period, according to the proper genius and circumstances of peoples and the requirements of the liturgy. The liturgical music of our own day, from every culture and region, should also serve the gathered assembly and its worship with due reverence and honor.[55]

42. When liturgical musicis chosen, the music itself, the text, and the ritual function should all be considered. Concerning the liturgical music, factors include the quality of composition; its ability to express the tone, content, and form of a text (for example, an acclamation or a hymn); and the ease with which it can be remembered and sung. A text may be prescribed (for example, the *Sanctus*) or freely chosen (for example, a liturgical song for the communion procession). Finally, regarding the ritual function, liturgical music may be an accompaniment to

---

54   See SC, no. 112.
55   See SC, nos. 112, 123

an action (for example, a procession) or a constitutive element of the rite (for example, the memorial acclamation).[56]

- The primary sources for the texts of the liturgical music are Scripture and the prayers and other texts of the liturgy. All such texts should bear the approval of the Church.[57]

- Liturgical music is provided in the *Roman Missal* as a model, especially when singing will be unaccompanied. Local composers will create suitable settings appropriate to the culture and traditions of the people.

- Many forms of liturgical music are employed in the liturgy according to the nature of the various components of the rites: for example, the responsorial form, acclamations, responses, and hymns.

43. Outside the seasons of Advent, Lent, and the Easter Triduum, and at services and Masses for the Dead, instrumental music may be employed to lend a reflective tone to the celebration and especially to create an atmosphere conducive to recollection and quiet prayer.[58] While the organ is to be accorded pride of place, other wind, string, or percussion instruments may be used in liturgical services in the dioceses of the United

---

56   See GIRM, nos. 39-41.
57   See GIRM, no. 48; see DD, no. 50.
58   See MusSacr, no. 66.

States of America, according to long-standing local usage, provided they are truly apt for sacred use or can be rendered apt.

44. While liturgical music is integral to every liturgical celebration, not every liturgy is celebrated with the same degree of solemnity. Sundays and holy days of obligation, as well as other solemnities, are of the first importance and demand greater preparation. Other celebrations are planned in light of the community's needs and resources.

45. It is important that the liturgical music chosen reflect the nature of the season or occasion, that it contribute to developing a stable repertoire, and that, if it will be used regularly, it be strong enough to bear repetition.

46. The selection of liturgical music begins with the liturgical texts themselves. Priority is given to singing the constitutive parts of the Mass in preference to hymns; among these parts, priority should be given to the Responsorial Psalm, to the acclamations before the Gospel and within the Eucharistic Prayer (for example, the *Sanctus* and acclamation after the consecration), the concluding Amen and the other presidential prayers, and to the dialogues between the priest and the people (for example, the preface dialogue and the final dismissal).[59] The description of the *Order of Mass* in this introduction (nos. 66-147) recommends which elements may or should be sung.

---

59   See LM, nos. 19-20; see GIRM, nos. 39-41; see MusSacr, nos. 7, 29.

Silence

47. Silence is, as in all communication, a most important element in the communication between God and the community of faith. Its purpose is to allow the voice of the Holy Spirit to be heard in the hearts of the People of God and to enable them to unite personal prayer more closely with the word of God and the public voice of the Church.[60] During liturgical silence, all respond in their own way: recollecting themselves, pondering what has been heard, petitioning and praising God in their inmost spirit.[61]

48. Liturgical silence is not merely an absence of words, a pause, or an interlude. Rather, it is a stillness, a quieting of spirits, a taking of time and leisure to hear, assimilate, and respond. Any haste that hinders reflectiveness should be avoided. The dialogue between God and the community of faith taking place through the Holy Spirit requires intervals of silence, suited to the congregation, so that all can take to heart the word of God and respond to it in prayer.[62]

- At the beginning of the rite of blessing and sprinkling of water, the people pause to ask for God's blessing on the water as a sign of Baptism. In the penitential rite, they pause to remember their sinfulness and the loving kindness of God in Christ. At the Opening Prayer, they put themselves and their deepest needs and desires before

60   See SC, no. 30; see GILH, no. 202; see EP, no. 18.
61   See EP, no. 18.
62   See LM, no. 28.

God. After the readings and homily, they savor the inspired word, ponder it in their hearts as Mary did (see Lk 2:19), and apply it to their lives. Before Holy Communion, they prepare themselves to receive the Lord and afterward praise God in silent prayer.[63]

- Liturgical silence is a corporate activity which is shared by all present and in which all support and sustain each other in profound prayerful solidarity. It demands a stillness and prayerful concentration, which the priest celebrant and everyone can help to create.

- Structurally, liturgical silence is indispensable to the rhythm of a balanced celebration. Without it the celebration can become perfunctory in its haste or burdensome in its unrelieved sound and song.

Materials and Objects

49. Materials and objects used in the Eucharist are to be "truly worthy and beautiful," authentic in their noble simplicity, and well adapted to sacred use.[64] The greatest care and sensitivity are necessary, even in the smallest matters, to achieve a "noble simplicity" and elegance.[65] In the choice of materials for sacred furnishings, nontraditional materials are acceptable if by contemporary standards they are considered to be noble, are durable, and are well suited for sacred use. In the dioceses of

---

63   See GIRM, no. 45.
64   GIRM, no. 288; see GIRM, nos. 325-326.
65   GIRM, no. 351.

the United States of America, these materials may include wood, stone, or metal, which are solid and appropriate to the purpose for which they are employed. These following paragraphs (nos. 50-58) refer to the actual celebration of the Eucharist and the principal materials and objects used in it.

BREAD AND WINE

50. The very nature of sacramental symbolism demands that the elements for the Eucharist be recognizable, in themselves and without explanation, as food and drink, while the authenticity of sacramental celebration demands that the elements for the Eucharist follow the unvarying tradition of the Latin Church.

- Bread should be recently made from wheat flour, should be unleavened and free from any foreign substance, and should "have the appearance of food."[66] In other words, it should be identifiable as bread by means of its consistency— that is, its color, taste, texture, and smell—while its form should remain the traditional one.[67]

- Wine should be natural and pure, the fermented juice of the grape, and similarly free from any foreign substance.[68]

SACRED VESSELS

51. Sacred Vessels for the Eucharistic elements should be made of noble metals, gilded on the inside unless they are made of

---

66   GIRM, no. 321.
67   See ID, no. 8.
68   See GIRM, no. 322.

gold or a more noble metal, in a form consistent with local usage and with their function in the liturgy.[69] They should be clearly distinguishable from objects in everyday use and be reserved exclusively for the liturgy. In the dioceses of the United States of America, Sacred Vessels may also be made from other solid materials that, according to the common estimation in each region, are precious—for example, ebony or other hard woods—provided that such materials are suitable for sacred use and do not break easily or deteriorate. This applies to all vessels that hold the hosts: such as the paten, the ciborium, the pyx, the monstrance, and so on.

• The fundamental Eucharistic symbolism of many sharing in the one bread and one cup is more clearly expressed when all the bread is contained in a single vessel and all the wine in one vessel. Until the chalice is brought to the altar for the Preparation of the Gifts, it is fittingly covered with a veil, which may be white or else the color of the day.[70] Additional Sacred Vessels may be necessary for the distribution of Holy Communion and may be brought to the altar at the breaking of the bread.

• Sacred Vessels for the distribution of the Body of Christ preferably have the form of patens and ciboria rather than of chalices. Chalices for the Blood of Christ need to be

---

69   See GIRM, nos. 328-329.
70   See GIRM, no. 118.

large enough to be shared, easily handled between minister and communicant, and easily tilted by the communicant for drinking.

• A suitable pitcher and basin may be used for the washing of the priest's hands. The water intended to be mixed with the wine should be contained in a smaller, separate vessel appropriate for that purpose. Generous quantities of water and a towel will be necessary if the priest is to do more than wet the tips of his fingers.

ALTAR

52. "The altar on which the Sacrifice of the Cross is made present under sacramental signs is also the table of the Lord to which the People of God is called together to participate in the Mass, as well as the center of the thanksgiving that is accomplished through the Eucharist."[71]

• The design of the altar reflects its place as the focus of attention during the Liturgy of the Eucharist as well as reflecting its function. In keeping with the Church's traditional practice and the altar's symbolism, the table of a fixed altar is to be made of stone—indeed, of natural stone. In the dioceses of the United States of America, however, wood that is worthy, solid, and well crafted may be used, provided that the altar is structurally immobile.

---

71   GIRM, no. 296; see BLS, nos. 56-60.

Its size and proportions should be appropriate to the normal Sunday Eucharistic celebration, and it should be able to accommodate the patens, ciboria, and chalices for the Communion of the faithful.

• Out of respect for Christ's memorial banquet, the altar is adorned with a covering both during and after Mass.[72] This cover may be a cloth that covers only the top of the altar, or it may envelop the altar more fully. While the principal altar cloth is to be white, other cloths of colors that possess special religious, honorific, or festive significance according to long-standing local usage may be employed, or frontals may also be used. However, the uppermost cloth covering the mensa (i.e., the altar cloth itself) is always white in color. The shape, size, and decoration of the altar cloth should be in keeping with the design of the altar. The fabric for altar cloths should be of good quality, design, and texture. At the Preparation of the Gifts, one or more corporals—large enough to accommodate the Sacred Vessels brought to the altar at the Preparation of the Gifts—are spread on top of the altar.

• Candles are used to express both reverence and festivity. They should be authentic and be made of a substance that gives a living flame and is seen to be consumed in giving its light. The candles may be placed on the altar or, more appropriately, near or around it, so as not to distract from

---

72   See GIRM, no. 304.

the Sacred Vessels or impede the participants' view of the liturgical action.[73]

- The top of the altar itself holds only what is necessary for the celebration—for example, the Sacred Vessels and *Roman Missal*—and those things remain on the altar only while needed. Decorative items like flowers may be placed near or around the altar, but not on it.

AMBO

53. When the Scriptures are read in church, God speaks to his people, and in the proclamation of the Gospel reading Christ himself is present in his word. The place from which the Scriptures are proclaimed is regarded as the "table of God's word" and is therefore a symbol of the surpassing dignity of that word.[74]

- In accord with its dignity, the ambo is used exclusively for the proclamation of God's word in the Scriptures, including the singing of the Responsorial Psalm, the elucidation and application of the word in the homily and Prayers of the Faithful, and also the Easter proclamation (*Exsultet*).[75]

- The design of the ambo reflects its place as the focus of attention during the Liturgy of the Word and its function.

---

73 See GIRM, no. 307; see BLS, no. 92.
74 LM, no. 32; see GIRM, no. 29; see BLS, nos. 61-62.
75 See LM, no. 33.

The ambo is to be somewhat elevated, fixed, and of noble design, in "harmonious and close relationship . . . with the altar."[76]

CHAIR

54. Christ is present in the person of the Bishop or priest who presides at the liturgy. The chair stands as a sign of his office, especially with regard to the Bishop. It symbolizes unity, leadership, and service to the gathered assembly. Its position allows the priest to be seen easily and heard by all. Anything resembling a throne is to be avoided.[77]

• From the chair, the priest leads the introductory and concluding rites and presides over the Liturgy of the Word. He may also give the homily and say the Prayer After Communion while standing at the chair.[78]

• When the priest and ministers move from chair to ambo or to altar, the different parts of the Mass are more clearly distinguished, and the presence of the Lord in word and sacrament is more effectively conveyed.

CROSS

55. The Paschal Mystery celebrated in the Eucharistic liturgy was accomplished through the crucifixion and resurrection.

---

76   LM, no. 32; see GIRM, no. 309
77   See GIRM, nos. 27, 310; see BLS, nos. 63-65.
78   See GIRM, nos. 124, 165; see LM, no. 26.

Christians glory in the cross of the Lord (see Gal 6:14). As a constant reminder of the cost of salvation and the symbol of Christian hope, the cross adorned with the image of the crucified Lord should be visible to all both during and after the celebration of the Eucharist. It may be carried in procession, or a cross may be permanently fixed on or near the altar.[79] Care should be taken not to multiply crosses in the place of worship and so detract from the effect of this symbol of the Paschal Mystery. Crosses in the Church may be covered from the conclusion of the Mass for Saturday of the Fourth Weeek of Lent until the end of the celebration of the Lord's Passion on Good Friday. Images in the Church may be covered from the conclusion of the Mass for Saturday of the Fourth Week of Lent until the beginning of the Easter Vigil.

BOOKS

56. The books used in the celebration of the Eucharist serve to communicate God's presence to us in the word or to articulate the Church's response to God in praise and adoration. In both capacities they facilitate the action of Christ in the Church.[80]

• The books from which the word of God is proclaimed (*Lectionary for Mass* and *Book of the Gospels*) are treated with veneration. They need to be of large size, strong binding, and noble design. Other books, including the *Roman Missal*, while worthy, need not draw attention and should

---

79   See GIRM, nos. 122, 308; see BLS, no. 91.
80   See LM, no. 35.

not be carried in procession. Pamphlets and leaflets detract from the visual integrity of the total liturgical action and should never be used in the exercise of the various roles in the liturgy.[81] Instead, to enable the full and active participation of the faithful, suitable books containing the music and other necessary texts may need to be provided.

VESTURE

57. Vestments serve several functions in the celebration of the Eucharist. As festal clothing, for example, they suggest the ritual and solemn character of the Eucharistic banquet, and as insignia, they identify the specific function or ministry of those who wear them.[82]

- The garment common to all ministers is the alb, which can express unity and enhance the visual dignity of the celebration. The form and design of the alb should complement the ritual and festive character of the celebration. Unless the design of the alb suggests otherwise or already covers non-liturgical clothing adequately, an amice and cincture should also be worn.

- The chasuble, worn over the alb and stole, is the proper vestment of the priest. It may be made from either natural or synthetic fabrics that are worthy and beautiful. Beauty

---

81   See LM, no. 37.
82   See GIRM, no. 335; see BLS, nos. 164-165.

should derive from the quality and cut of the fabric as much as from its ornamentation.[83]

- Concelebrating priests wear either a chasuble over the alb and stole, an alb and stole alone or a chasuble-alb and stole. Vestments that differ in size, shape, and ornamentation can obscure unity, emphasize individualism, and detract from the presidential role of the presiding priest.

- The deacon wears an amice, alb, cincture, stole, and dalmatic; but the dalmatic may be omitted.[84]

- In the dioceses of the United States of America, acolytes, altar servers, lectors, and other lay ministers may wear the alb or other appropriate and dignified clothing.[85]

- In the United States of America, white, violet, or black vestments may be used for the celebration of the funeral liturgy or Masses for the Dead.[86] Gold- or silver-colored vestments may be worn at more solemn occasions in the dioceses of the United States of America.

- In the United States of America, the chasuble-alb, worn with a stole, may be used by the priest instead of the usual

---

83   See GIRM, nos. 337, 343, 344; see GCE, no. 14.
84   See GIRM, nos. 119, 336, 338.
85   See GIRM, no. 339.
86   See GIRM, no. 346

vestments in the following circumstances: in concelebrations (when he is not the principal concelebrant); in Masses for special groups; in celebrations outside a sacred place; and in similar situations in which, due to place or persons, its use seems advisable. In these circumstances only the stole need be the color the day. On all other occasions the priest celebrant wears the complete set of vestments for Mass, all of one color.[87]

INCENSE

58. Incense has been used since before Christian times both as a sign of respect and honor and as a symbol of prayer rising before God. Incense suggests both the otherness of the transcendent God and the cloud that symbolized God's glory and presence in the midst of the Israelites. It can contribute powerfully to a sense of mystery. As a sweet-smelling aroma, it represents the prayers of the Church rising before God as an acceptable oblation (see 141:2 and Rev 8:4).

- Incense that, when burning, appeals to our sight and our sense of smell should be used in amounts sufficient to be readily seen and smelled.

- In the introductory rites, incense may be carried in the entrance procession and used at the veneration of the altar

---

87   Indult granted to the dioceses of the United States of America, May 11, 1977.

and cross. In the Liturgy of the Word, it may be carried in the Gospel procession and used to venerate the *Book of the Gospels*. In the Liturgy of the Eucharist, it may be used at the Preparation of the Gifts to honor the elements and the altar and to acknowledge the presence and action of Christ in the priest celebrant and the other members of the liturgical assembly. It may also be used at the showing of the Eucharistic bread and the chalice after the consecration.[88]

• The use of incense at any or all of these points is optional; its use at any one point does not necessitate its use at all the others. It is used in order to express the solemnity of a particular celebration or to enhance a particular moment within a celebration.

ADAPTING THE CELEBRATION TO PARTICULAR CIRCUMSTANCES

59. While great importance should be attached to any Mass celebrated with a community, this is particularly true of the parish celebration of the Lord's Day, which is the typical expression of the Eucharist. Such celebrations assume the full, conscious, and active participation of the parish community,

---

88   See GIRM, no. 276.

the availability of all necessary resources, and a range of ministers and liturgical musicians.[89]

60. But if every Mass were celebrated in identical form and with the same degree of solemnity, then the Sunday celebration would cease to be truly preeminent. The revised liturgical books clearly presuppose that every celebration, in whatever circumstances, will fully consider the needs, capabilities, and situation of the community that assembles for it.[90] Days or periods of prayer for the fruits of the earth, prayer for human rights and equality, prayer for world justice and peace, and penitential observances outside Lent are to be observed in the dioceses of the United States of America at times to be designated by the diocesan Bishop. In all dioceses of the United States of America, January 22 (or January 23, when January 22 falls on a Sunday) shall be observed as a particular day of penance for violations to the dignity of the human person committed through acts of abortion and a day of prayer for the full restoration of the legal guarantee to the right to life. For this day, the Mass for "Peace and Justice" (no. 21 from "Masses for Various Needs") should be celebrated with violet vestments as an appropriate liturgical observance.

61. The liturgical celebrations of culturally and ethnically mixed groups require special attention. Weekday Masses; celebrations with smaller groups; celebrations outside churches or

---

89   See GIRM, nos. 113, 115, 116.
90   See GIRM, no. 352.

chapels; Masses with children, young people, the sick, or persons with disabilities; and ritual Masses (for example, funeral or wedding Masses) at which a significant number of the congregation may be non-Catholics or otherwise not able in law to receive Holy Communion[91] will necessarily impose different demands appropriate to the needs of the occasion.

In order to make clear the law of the Church on this matter, the Bishops of the United States of America issued in 1997 the following guidelines for receiving Holy Communion:

> **For Catholics**—As Catholics, we fully participate in the celebration of the Eucharist when we receive Holy Communion. We are encouraged to receive Communion devoutly and frequently. In order to be properly disposed to receive Communion, participants should not be conscious of grave sin and normally should have fasted for one hour. A person who is conscious of grave sin is not to receive the Body and Blood of the Lord without prior sacramental confession except for a grave reason when there is no opportunity for confession. In this case, the person is to be mindful of the obligation to make an act of perfect contrition, including the intention of confessing as soon as possible (see CIC, c. 916). A frequent reception of the sacrament of Penance is encouraged for all.

---

91   See CIC, c. 844.

For our fellow Christians—We welcome our fellow Christians to this celebration of the Eucharist as our brothers and sisters. We pray that our common Baptism and the action of the Holy Spirit in this Eucharist will draw us closer to one another and begin to dispel the sad divisions which separate us. We pray that these will lessen and finally disappear, in keeping with Christ's prayer for us "that they may all be one" (Jn 17:21).

Because Catholics believe that the celebration of the Eucharist is a sign of the reality of oneness of faith, life, and worship, members of these churches with whom we are not yet fully united are ordinarily not admitted to Holy Communion. Eucharistic sharing in exceptional circumstances by other Christians requires permission according to the directives of the diocesan Bishop and the provisions of canon law (c. 844 §4). Members of the Orthodox Churches, the Assyrian Church of the East, and the Polish National Catholic Church are urged to respect the discipline of their own Churches. According to Roman Catholic discipline, the Code of Canon Law does not object to the reception of Communion by Christians of these Churches (c. 844 §3).

For those not receiving Holy Communion—All who are not receiving Holy Communion are encouraged to express in their hearts prayerful desire for unity with the Lord Jesus and with one another.

For non-Christians—We would welcome to this celebration those who do not share our faith in Jesus Christ. While we cannot admit them to Holy Communion, we ask them to offer their prayers for the peace and unity of the human family.

62. Useful principles for adaptation or accommodation are suggested in the Roman Ritual for the rites of other sacraments, in the *Liturgy of the Hours*, and, more explicitly, in the *Directory for Masses with Children*. Some principles are also included in the *General Instruction of the Roman Missal* and in the *Order of Mass* itself.

63. The *General Instruction of the Liturgy of the Hours* articulates the principle of "progressive solemnity," which recognizes that the various parts of a liturgical celebration are not all of equal importance and require varying treatment, according to the significance of the day or hour being celebrated, the purpose of the various hours, the number and character of the community, and the number of available singers.[92]

64. The *Directory for Masses with Children* recognizes that Mass may occasionally need to be accommodated to the needs of children when they constitute the major proportion of the congregation. This does not suggest composing rites that are altogether special or different from the *Order of Mass* as it is usually celebrated. One of the purposes of specially prepared Masses for

---

92   See GILH, no. 273.

children is to lead the children to the celebration of Mass with adults, particularly the Sunday Mass of the parish community.[93]

One of the prescribed Eucharistic Prayers for Children may be used at Masses celebrated for children alone or at which the majority of the participants are children who have not yet reached the age of preadolescence. These prayers are intended to help achieve the active participation of children in the Eucharistic Prayer, the Church's central prayer of praise and thanksgiving (see nos. 111-124). In language and their treatment of Eucharistic themes, these Eucharistic Prayers are suited for use with children ranging from early school age to preadolescence.[94]

65. Some limited examples of the kinds of accommodations that may be considered include the following:

- When an antiphon cannot be used according to its original purpose as a chant or processional refrain, it may be better used in other ways. For example, the opening antiphon could be used to provide a theme for an introductory admonition. Similarly, when the communion antiphon cannot be sung, using it as a focus for the period of silence after Communion may be preferable.[95]

---

93   See DMC, nos. 19, 21.
94   See EPMC, nos. 14-15.
95   See CP, no. 40a.

- At celebrations planned for children, approved adaptations of the *Gloria*, Profession of Faith (Creed), *Sanctus*, and *Agnus Dei* may be used, if they help to encourage the children's readier participation. But great care must be taken to ensure that these adaptations completely respect the meaning of the originals and their functions in the rite. Such paraphrases should not be used at adult celebrations.[96]

---

96   See DMC, no. 31.

II.

INTRODUCTORY RITES

66. In the introductory rites, Christ joins the Church to himself and gathers her children to join their voices to his perfect hymn of praise. Thus, the liturgical assembly, "where two or three come together in Christ's name, and where he is found in their midst (see Mt 18:20), is the 'first image that the Church gives of herself.'"[97] Thus an important function of these rites is to enable the gathered assembly to take on the form of a community, alert and ready to listen to the word and to celebrate the sacrament.[98]

The introductory rites are led from the chair rather than from the altar or ambo unless otherwise prescribed in the liturgical books for specific times and circumstances.[99]

Entrance Procession

67. Worship begins with the opening song and procession, which help to create an ambience of solemnity, a sense of oneness in Christ, and an awareness of the mystery being unfolded.[100]

---

97   Pope John Paul II, Allocution *Chers frères dans l'épiscopat* (March 8, 1997), no. 5.
98   See SC, no. 7; see GIRM, nos. 7, 24; see CCC, nos. 1366-1367.
99   See GIRM, no. 124.
100   See GIRM, no. 47.

- The opening song should be one that everyone is able to join in singing to some degree. It may consist of any of the following: an antiphon and psalm from the *Roman Missal* as set to music by the *Roman Gradual* or another musical setting; the seasonal antiphon and psalm of the *Simple Gradual*; a song from another collection of psalms and antiphons approved by the USCCB or the diocesan Bishop, including psalms arranged in responsorial or metrical forms; or a suitable liturgical song chosen in accordance with GIRM, paragraph no. 47. When no singing is possible, the recommended antiphon may appropriately be used by incorporating it into the introductory remarks that may follow the greeting.[101]

- A procession of the priest celebrant and the other ministers through the congregation expresses visibly the unity and fullness of the assembly.

- Depending on the occasion, the procession is led by servers carrying the censer with burning incense, the cross, and two candles. They are followed by acolytes and other liturgical ministers, then the deacon or lector carrying the *Book of the Gospels*, if it is to be used. Concelebrants, the deacon of the Mass, and the priest celebrant then follow. If the *Book of the Gospels* has been carried, it is placed on the altar upon arrival in the sanctuary.

---

101   See GIRM, no. 48; see CP, no. 40a.

68. The altar is an abiding symbol of Christ and the center of the Eucharistic action.[102]

- The priest and deacon, together with concelebrants and other ministers in the procession, bow to the altar on arrival as a sign of reverence. If a tabernacle containing the blessed sacrament is behind or near the altar, they genuflect.[103] However, those who are carrying a liturgical object (for example, a cross, book, or candle) do not genuflect. Afterward, the priest, deacon, and any concelebrants make an additional reverence to the altar with a kiss.[104]

- On more solemn occasions, this reverence may be enhanced by the use of incense.[105]

- After the procession and the reverencing of the altar, the priest and deacon proceed to the chair. From there the priest greets the people and leads the opening rite.[106]

Greeting

69. After making the Sign of the Cross together, the priest and people exchange formal greetings as a mutual acknowledgement and evocation of the presence of Christ in their midst

---

102   See EuchMyst, no. 24.
103   See GIRM, no. 122.
104   See GIRM, nos. 49, 122, 123, 173, 275b.
105   See GIRM, no. 123.
106   See GIRM, nos. 124, 174.

and as a prayer for his sustaining power.[107] As the first dialogue between priest and people, the greeting and response should be both warm and reverent. Casual and personalized greetings that emphasize a merely human exchange and obscure the mystery of Christ's presence and action are inappropriate.

70. The Mass of the day may be introduced at this point. A brief and well-prepared comment can help to create the appropriate atmosphere and give tone and orientation to the entire celebration.[108] Though the introduction is normally the function of the priest, on occasion it may be fitting for the deacon or some other member of the congregation to do this.

At this point, strangers, guests, and special groups may briefly be welcomed to the celebration. When significant numbers of children are present, they may be acknowledged and addressed directly at this point.[109]

Act of Penance

71. One of the texts provided in the *Roman Missal* can be chosen for the Act of Penance; alternatively, in a Mass celebrated on Sunday, the Order for the Blessing and Sprinkling of Holy Water may occasionally replace the Act of Penance. The choice or composition of texts for the Act of Penance may be made on

---

107   See GIRM, no. 50.
108   See GIRM, no. 50; see EP, no. 14.
109   See DMC, no. 17.

the basis of the liturgical season, the feast, the particular occasion (for example, a particular ritual Mass), or the circumstances of the congregation that gathers for the celebration. Each of the forms provided begins with an invitation by the priest, who may use one of the formularies provided or (where this is foreseen by the rubrics) his own words. On occasion, the invitation may appropriately be incorporated into the introductory remarks that may follow the greeting.

72. In the Act of Penance, the faithful, gathered in God's presence, recognize their sinfulness and confess the mystery of Christ's love. This may take one of two forms, both of which conclude with a prayer of absolution.

a.   The first form, once a private prayer of preparation, is a general confession that invokes the support of the communion of saints and, specifically, of the community gathered for the Eucharist.

b.   The second form comprises verses of the penitential psalms.

73. The *Kyrie* is an ancient chant by which all present acclaim the Lord and plead for his mercy.[110] The Roman Church adapted it from the Greek liturgies. It may be used in English or in the original Greek. It is by nature a chant and, when used, is normally sung by all, alternating with the cantor or choir.

---

110   See GIRM, no. 52.

Rite of Blessing and Sprinkling of Water

74. As they assemble, the People of God are attentive to the risen Christ. In so doing, they recognize themselves both as reconciled sinners and as those in need of forgiveness of personal sins committed daily. The blessing and sprinkling of water serves as a memorial of Easter and Baptism. God is thanked for intervening to save us through the medium of water and is asked to continue to give forgiveness and life.

- Because of its emphasis on Easter and Baptism, on occasion the blessing and sprinkling may appropriately be done during the season of Easter.

- If the greeting and blessing take place at the door, the priest may sprinkle the people during the entrance procession.

- So that the rite of sprinkling may clearly point to a renewal of the cleansing waters of Baptism, a sufficient amount of water should be used.

GLORIA

75. The *Gloria* is one of the Church's most ancient, solemn hymns. The *Gloria* is by nature a festive hymn and should be sung by the whole congregation, alternately with the choir, or by the choir alone.[111] Every effort should be made to ensure that the *Gloria* can be sung; however, for pastoral reasons it may be recited instead.

---

111   See GIRM, no. 53.

- No other text or song may be substituted for the *Gloria*.[112]

- The *Gloria* is sung or said on Sundays outside Advent and Lent, on solemnities and feasts, and in more solemn celebrations.[113]

OTHER OPENING RITES

76. Certain other opening rites are prescribed in the respective liturgical books for particular celebrations and occasions. These rites occur on certain special feasts, when the Liturgy of the Hours is combined with the Mass, or when special rites are celebrated during the Mass: for example, Baptism, Marriage, or funeral rites. Sometimes—for example, on Passion Sunday or on the Feast of the Presentation of the Lord—when an entrance procession forms part of the opening rite itself, the opening rite follows the form given for these occasions.

Opening Prayer (Collect)

77. The Collect, or Opening Prayer, completes the introductory rites. Through petition to God, it sets the tone of the celebration and prepares all present to hear the word of God.[114]

- As the culmination of the introductory rites, a Collect is always used. It may be sung or said.

---

112 See GIRM, no. 53.
113 See GIRM, no. 53.
114 See GIRM, no. 54.

- When paraphrases are permitted at Masses with children, they should respect the nature of this prayer.[115]

- After the invitation "Let us pray," all observe some moments of silence in which they place themselves in God's presence and pray.

- The Collect always ends with the longer Trinitarian conclusion, to which the congregation responds, "Amen."

---

115 See DMC, no. 51.

III.

LITURGY

OF THE WORD

78. The Mass is made up of the Liturgy of the Word and the Liturgy of the Eucharist, which are so closely connected as to form one act of worship. In the word of God, the divine covenant is announced; in the Eucharist, the new and everlasting covenant is embodied and renewed.[116]

79. The chosen people entered into a special covenant with God at Sinai, one that was renewed and fulfilled on Calvary. By hearing the word proclaimed in worship, the faithful enter into the dialogue between God and the covenant people, a dialogue sealed in the sharing of the Eucharist. The meaning of communion is proclaimed in the word; the presence of Christ in the proclamation of the word is made actual once again in the banquet of Holy Communion. The proclamation of the word is thus integral to the Mass and lies at its very heart.

80. The proper celebration of the Liturgy of the Word involves many elements and several of the faithful, but care must be taken so that the many human words and elements do not obscure the divine word itself. In this dialogue with the Lord,

---

116 See GIRM, no. 28; see LM, no. 10.

the people listen to the word, reflect on it in silence, respond to it in song, assimilate it, and apply it to their lives. Moved by it, they profess their faith and intercede for the needs of the Church and the world.

81. The *Lectionary for Mass*, revised at the direction of the Second Vatican Council, has opened up the treasures of the Bible, so that richer fare might be provided for the faithful at the table of God's word.[117] The Introduction to the *Lectionary* speaks extensively of the word of God in the plan of salvation and in the life of the Church. In particular, those who assist in liturgical roles pertaining to the Liturgy of the Word will want to study this introduction and take its teaching to heart.

82. The various liturgical roles of the Liturgy of the Word and guidelines for their service are given in the Introduction to the *Lectionary for Mass* and in the first part of this introduction to the *Order of Mass*.

Biblical Readings

83. In the word of God handed down in the Scriptures, the community of faith even now hears God speaking to it. For this reason the biblical readings and their accompanying Scripture chants may not be omitted, shortened, or replaced by non-biblical texts.[118]

---

117 See SC, no. 51.
118 See GIRM, no. 55; see LM, no. 12.

- On occasion, shortened readings are provided in the *Lectionary for Mass*; however, in the absence of a true pastoral reason, the entire text is to be read.

- The readings are always proclaimed from the ambo.[119]

84. The proclamation of the Gospel reading is the high point of the Liturgy of the Word. The other readings in their established sequence from the Old and New Testaments prepare all present for this proclamation.[120]

85. The principles governing the selection and distribution of these readings are explained in the Introduction to the *Lectionary*. The adaptations to the *Ordo Lectionum Missae* as contained in the *Lectionary for Mass for Use in the Dioceses of the United States of America* should be carefully observed.

- The observance of a prayerful silence is recommended after the first and second readings and again after the homily.[121]

- The Liturgy of the Word may be introduced by a brief word on the background of the readings, when doing so would be helpful. Such comments, whether from the priest or another minister, should always be succinct and well prepared.[122]

---

119   See GIRM, no. 58.
120   See LM, no. 13.
121   See GIRM, no. 56.
122   See LM, no. 31.

- The readings may be sung, provided that the form of singing respects the rhythms and genius of the language and does not obscure the words.

- The conclusion "The word of the Lord" after the first and second readings may be sung, even by someone other than the lector, so as to elicit from the faithful a sung response of gratitude for the word of God.[123]

Responsorial Psalm

86. The Responsorial Psalm follows the first reading and is an integral part of the Liturgy of the Word. After hearing and taking to heart God's word, all respond with words that are themselves God-given. Words that have expressed the faith of God's people over the centuries are selected by the Church to express the appropriate response, whether of wonder and praise, repentance and sorrow, hope and trust, or joy and exultation.

87. All present are to be helped and encouraged to discern God's word in the psalms, to adopt them as their own prayer, and to experience them as the prayer of the Church.

- The psalms, the songs and hymns of Israel, are normally sung. This may be done in a variety of ways. The preferred form is responsorial, in which the psalmist or cantor sings the verses and the whole congregation takes up the response. The direct form, also permitted, has no interven-

---

123   See LM, no. 18.

ing response, and the cantor, or all together, sing the verses consecutively.[124] But if other ways of singing or sharing the psalms are appropriate to the particular language or culture, they too are used, so that the people's participation may be facilitated by every means.[125]

- Even when singing the psalm is impossible, it should be recited in a manner conducive to meditation.[126]

- In the dioceses of the United States of America, the following may also be sung in place of the psalms assigned in the *Lectionary for Mass*: either the proper or seasonal antiphon and psalm from the *Lectionary*, set either in the manner of the *Roman* or *Simple Gradual* or in another musical setting; or an antiphon and psalm from another collection of the psalms and antiphons, including psalms arranged in metrical form, providing that they have been approved by the USCCB or the diocesan Bishop. Songs or hymns may not be used in place of the Responsorial Psalm.[127]

Gospel Acclamation

88. The Alleluia or, according to the season, the Gospel Acclamation is an acclamation that expresses the people's greeting of the Lord and their faith in his presence as he addresses them in the Gospel reading.[128]

---

124   See LM, no. 20.
125   See LM, no. 21.
126   See LM, no. 22.
127   See GIRM, no. 61; see LM, no. 89.
128   See LM, no. 23.

89. The Gospel Acclamation has traditionally accompanied the Gospel procession, in which the *Book of the Gospels* is carried to the ambo accompanied by lights and incense.

- The Alleluia or Gospel Acclamation looks forward to the Gospel reading. It does not respond to the previous reading, from which it is separated by a distinct pause.

- If incense is to be used at the Gospel reading, it is prepared after the second reading and before the Gospel procession.

- The deacon who is to proclaim the Gospel reading bows before the priest celebrant and asks for a blessing. If a priest reads the Gospel, he bows before the altar and silently recites the prescribed prayer.

- All stand while the procession moves to the ambo and the Alleluia or acclamation is sung.

- As an acclamation, the Alleluia or Gospel Acclamation is sung by everyone present and may be repeated as appropriate. The verse may be sung by cantor or choir (or even recited). If the acclamation cannot be sung, it may be omitted.[129]

---

129   See LM, no. 23; see GIRM, no. 63c.

Sequence

90. The Sequence is an ancient liturgical component of great textual and musical beauty. With the exception of those of Easter and Pentecost, the Sequences currently found in the *Roman Missal* are optional. When used, the Sequence follows the Alleluia.[130]

Gospel Reading

91. Because the proclamation of the Gospel reading is the high point of the Liturgy of the Word, it is distinguished from the other readings by special marks of honor. Its proclamation is reserved to a deacon or, in his absence, a priest. The one who proclaims the Gospel reading prepares himself: the deacon by receiving a blessing, the priest by reciting the prescribed prayer. The people stand to hear the Gospel reading and acclaim Christ present and speaking to them. Servers with candles may stand on each side of the ambo, and the book may be incensed before the text is proclaimed. If the *Book of the Gospels* is used, it is carried in procession from the altar to the ambo.[131]

- The proclamation of the Gospel reading is never omitted, even at Masses with children at which an abbreviated Liturgy of the Word is permitted.[132]

---

130 See GIRM, no. 64.
131 See GIRM, nos. 133, 175.
132 See DMC, no. 42.

- The Gospel reading is proclaimed by a deacon. If no deacon is present, it is proclaimed as a rule by a priest other than the one presiding. If no deacon or other priest is present, it is to be read by the priest who presides.[133]

- With his hands joined, the deacon (or priest) greets the people with "The Lord be with you"; and while announcing the Gospel passage, he makes the Sign of the Cross, first on the book and then on his forehead, lips, and breast. The faithful also sign themselves in this way and then respond, "Glory to you, Lord."[134]

- Even if the Gospel reading itself is not sung, singing the greeting and title of the Gospel reading at the beginning and likewise "The Gospel of the Lord" at the end will allow the people to sing their acclamation.[135]

Homily

92. The homily is an integral part of the liturgy and a necessary source of nourishment for the Christian life. By means of the homily, the mysteries of the faith and the guiding principles of Christian living are expounded, most often from the Scriptures proclaimed but also from the other texts and rites of the liturgy.[136]

---

133   See GIRM, no. 59 .
134   See GIRM, no. 134.
135   See LM, no. 65.
136   See GIRM, no. 29; see SC, no. 52.

93. In the readings, God's word is accessible to people of every age and condition, but the homily as a living explanation of the word increases its impact by assisting the faithful in assimilating it and applying it in their lives. It leads them from contemplation of the word to profound appropriation of the mystery of Christ and his sacrifice in a more wholehearted celebration of the Eucharist and in their daily lives.[137]

94. If it is to fulfill its purpose, the homily must be the fruit of meditation, carefully prepared, and in length, style, and content sensitively adapted to the needs and capacities of all present.[138] This may be more easily achieved if the priest prepares the homily in shared reflection and prayer with members or representatives of the congregation.

- On Sundays and holy days of obligation a homily must be given at all Masses celebrated with a congregation; it may not be omitted without a serious reason.[139]

- A homily is strongly recommended on the weekdays of Advent, Christmas, Lent, and Easter and on other occasions when people come in considerable numbers. For the benefit of regular participants, and because it is indeed an integral part of the liturgy, a homily is appropriate at almost all Masses with a congregation.[140]

---

137 See GIRM, no. 65; see LM, no. 24.
138 See GIRM, nos. 69, 111, 352; see LM, no. 24.
139 See GIRM, no. 66; see LM, no. 25.
140 See LM, no. 25.

- The homily is reserved to a priest or deacon[141] and is ordinarily given by the priest who presides. A deacon or, at a concelebration, one of the concelebrating priests may be invited to preach.[142] In extraordinary circumstances, a Bishop or priest who is present but not concelebrating may be invited to preach the homily.[143]

- At Masses for children, an adult who is better able to communicate with children may be asked to speak after the Gospel reading.[144] Such preaching has its own importance, though it is not a homily. The one who gives the homily or speaks at this point should be a participant in the entire celebration and so experience the proclamation of the word on which the preaching is based and the consummation of the celebration in Eucharistic communion. In these Masses, the homilist may need to physically approach the congregation in order to communicate effectively.

- Other than at Masses for children, the priest celebrant gives the homily while standing at the ambo or at his chair.[145]

141   See CIC, c. 767 §1.
142   See GIRM, nos. 66, 94, 213.
143   See GIRM, no. 66.
144   See DMC, no. 24.
145   See LM, no. 26; see GIRM, no. 136.

- The custom of beginning and ending the homily with the Sign of the Cross arose when the sermon was somewhat detached from the Liturgy of the Mass. The practice is now not advised.[146]

- A period of silence following the homily is most appropriate, so that the people may take the word of God to heart and respond to it in prayer.[147]

- If catechumens are present, they may be kindly dismissed before the Profession of Faith (Creed) in order to go and reflect together on the word proclaimed. Texts for this dismissal are provided in the *Rite of Christian Initiation of Adults*.[148]

Profession of Faith (Creed)

95. In the Profession of Faith, or Creed, the people respond and assent to the word of God heard in the readings and the homily. And before they celebrate the mystery of faith in the Eucharist, they call to mind the rule of faith in a formulary approved by the Church.[149]

---

146 See Congregation for Divine Worship, Reply, *Notitiæ* 9 (1973) 178.
147 See LM, no. 28.
148 See RCIA, no. 67.
149 See LM, no. 29.

- The Profession of Faith is recited by priest and people together on Sundays and solemnities. It may also be said at other solemn celebrations.[150]

- The form customarily to be used is the Nicene Creed. The Apostles' Creed may replace the Nicene Creed at Masses with children and on Sundays of Lent and the Easter Season as the Church celebrates the mystery of the resurrection of Christ in the sacraments of initiation. No other Creeds may be used. Children, however, need to become accustomed to the Nicene Creed.

- At the Easter Vigil, and at Masses in which Baptism or Confirmation is celebrated, the Profession of Faith is replaced by the renewal of baptismal promises. The renewal of baptismal promises may also replace the Profession of Faith at the Masses of Easter Sunday.[151] In Masses that include acceptance into the order of catechumens and in ritual Masses for the election or enrollment of names or for the scrutinies, the Profession of Faith may be omitted.[152]

- Whether the Creed is sung or recited, this should be done in a way that involves all present.

---

150 See GIRM, no. 168.
151 See Renewal of Baptismal Promises, The Easter Vigil, p. 361, and Easter Day, p. 370.
152 See RCIA, nos. 68, 124, 143, 157, 164.

- All make a profound bow at the phrase that begins "By the power of the Holy Spirit," etc.; on the solemnities of the Annunciation and Christmas all kneel.

Prayer of the Faithful (Universal Prayer)

96. Enlightened and moved by God's word, all the baptized, gathered for worship by Christ the High Priest, share in his priestly intercession for all humanity. Because "the joys and hopes, the grief and anguish of the people of our time, especially of those who are poor or afflicted, are the joys and hopes, the grief and anguish of the followers of Christ as well,"[153] the Church prays for her own needs, for the salvation of the world, for civil authorities, for those oppressed by any burden, and for the local community, particularly those who are sick or who have died.[154]

97. Thus, even though the intentions may be quite concrete or particular in content, they should look beyond the concerns of the local congregation to the needs of the whole Church and of the wider world. In this way, they are a sign of the communion of the particular gathered assembly with the diocesan community and with the universal Church.

98. The priest celebrant directs the prayer from the chair. He briefly invites the people to pray, and at the end he draws their

---

153   GS, no. 1.
154   See LM, no. 30; see GIRM, nos. 69, 70.

intercessions together in a brief concluding prayer. The intentions are proposed by a deacon, another minister, or members of the congregation at the ambo or another suitable place. After each intention, the faithful respond by silent prayer, a common response, or both. They affirm the concluding prayer of the priest with their "Amen."[155]

- The Prayer of the Faithful is ordinarily included in all Masses.[156]

- Both the priest's introduction and the proposed intentions are addressed to the congregation, not to God. They are invitations or biddings to the faithful, who then pray for the suggested intention in the silence of their hearts and in a common petition.[157]

- These intentions should be short, clear, and objective enough for the faithful to comprehend and respond to them without difficulty. The response they are to evoke is petition rather than praise, thanksgiving, or repentance.

- On particular occasions, when other sacraments or particular rites are celebrated in conjunction with the Mass, the

---

155 See GIRM, no. 71; see LM, no. 31.
156 See GIRM, nos. 69, 264.
157 See GIRM, no. 71.

range of intentions may be more closely concerned with the occasion; but even so, the intentions should always include some that are general or universal.[158]

- For each intention, the invitation to pray and the response may be sung, or the entire intention may be sung.

- Those who propose the intentions return to their places only after the completion of the concluding prayer.

---

158   See GIRM, no. 70.

IV.

LITURGY

OF THE EUCHARIST

99. At the Last Supper, Christ instituted the sacrifice and paschal meal that make the sacrifice of the cross present in the Church. From the days of the Apostles the Church has celebrated that sacrifice by carrying out what the Lord did and handed over to his disciples to do in his memory. Like him, his priests have taken bread and wine, given thanks to God over them, broken the bread, and shared the bread and cup of blessing as the Body and Blood of Christ (see 1 Cor 10:16). The Eucharistic sacrifice, in all its rich variety of forms and traditions, has always retained this basic shape: the taking of the elements of bread and wine in the Preparation of the Gifts, the act of thanksgiving in the Eucharistic Prayer, the breaking of the bread, the giving and sharing of the Body and Blood of Christ in Holy Communion.[159]

PREPARATION OF THE GIFTS

100. At the beginning of the Liturgy of the Eucharist, the gifts that will become the Lord's Body and Blood are brought to the altar. This bringing of bread and wine is the Preparation of the

---

159   See GIRM, no. 72.

Gifts. It is not in itself the sacrifice or offering but is instead a preparation for the Eucharistic Prayer, the great act of blessing and thanksgiving that constitutes the Church's memorial offering of Christ's sacrifice, and for Holy Communion.[160]

101. The Church encourages the faithful to bring forward the elements through which Christ's offering will be made present, together with money and other gifts for the sustenance of Christ's body, especially the poor and the needy.

102. The purpose of this rite, then, is to make the altar, the gifts that are placed on it, and all who are present ready for the Eucharistic offering that follows.

Preparation of the Altar

103. First, the altar, the Lord's table, is prepared as the center of the Eucharistic liturgy.[161]

- Everything indicates that a new and important stage of the liturgy is about to begin. One or more corporals of sufficient size to accommodate all the Sacred Vessels that may be brought to the altar now are laid out.

- The corporal, purificators, and *Roman Missal* are needed for the Eucharistic offering. They are not themselves offerings or gifts and are not brought up in the procession of

---

160 See GIRM, no. 73.
161 See GIRM, no. 73.

gifts. Instead, they should be brought reverently but without ceremony from a side table, along with the chalice if it will be prepared at the altar.

- Since these are preparatory tasks, they are carried out by a deacon, acolyte, or other minister or by other members of the congregation.

Presentation of the Gifts

104. In the past, the people themselves provided the materials for the Eucharist. They also brought other foodstuffs to be blessed for their own use and for the poor. The rite of carrying up the gifts continues the spiritual value and meaning of the ancient custom. This is also the time to bring forward money or gifts for the poor and the Church.[162]

105. The procession with the gifts is a powerful expression of the participation of all present in the Eucharist and in the social mission of the Church. It is an expression of the humble and contrite heart, the dispossession of self that is necessary for making the true offering, which the Lord Jesus gave his people to make with him. The procession with the gifts expresses also our eager willingness to enter into the "holy exchange" with God: "accept the offerings you have given us, that we in turn may receive the gift of yourself."[163]

---

162   See GIRM, no. 73.
163   See December 29, Prayer Over the Offerings.

- The collection of money takes place first. As a part of the Eucharistic liturgy since apostolic times, its purpose and value will be better appreciated if, after the Prayer of the Faithful, the priest celebrant, ministers, and people all sit and wait while the collection is taken and then is made ready with the other gifts for the procession. The collection is not to be taken during the Profession of Faith or the Prayer of the Faithful, nor should it continue during the Prayer Over the Offerings or the Eucharistic Prayer. Music or song may begin with the collection and continue during the procession of gifts.

- The elements of bread and wine are carried in the procession in vessels that can be easily seen. If possible, the bread and wine should each be contained in a single vessel, so that priest and people may be seen to be sharing the same food and drink in the sacrament of unity.

- The gifts of bread, wine, and money are carried forward by members of the congregation. The congregation's identification with the gifts is best expressed if the procession passes right through their midst. The gifts are accepted by the priest, who may be assisted by the deacon and other ministers. The collection of money and other gifts is deposited near the altar or in another suitable place. The priest places only the Sacred Vessels containing the bread and wine on the altar.[164]

---

164   See GIRM, no. 73.

- In addition to money, gifts in kind and other real gifts for the poor are appropriate, but not token items that will be retrieved and returned to ordinary use after the celebration.

- The purpose of any music at this point is to accompany the collection, the procession, and the presentation of gifts, particularly when these will occupy a considerable period of time. Sung texts need not speak of bread and wine, nor of offering. Texts expressing joy, praise, community, as well as the spirit of the season, are appropriate. Since the presentation of gifts is preparatory, instrumental music or silence may also be effective.

Placing of the Gifts on the Altar

106. The formularies accompanying the placing of the gifts on the altar are reminiscent of Jewish table prayers. They are an expression of praise of God for the creation of the world since it is through his abundant goodness that every gift is bestowed upon all people, including these gifts of bread and wine, which by the will of God and at the hands of the priest will become the very Body and Blood of Jesus Christ.

- The priest holds the paten containing the bread slightly above the altar and praises God with the prayer of blessing over the bread. He places the bread on the altar. He then holds the chalice in the same way, blesses God with the prayer of blessing over the wine, and places the chalice on the altar.

- Since the taking of bread and wine is expressed primarily by the action, normally both blessings will be uttered inaudibly during the singing or music. If no music is being played, the priest may say them aloud. In this case, the people may respond with the acclamation "Blessed be God for ever." The two blessings should be seen as a unit; for one to be said inaudibly and the other aloud should never happen, nor should the two be joined into one prayer.

Mixing of Wine and Water

107. In the ancient world, wine was regularly tempered with water. In time this functional practice during the Eucharist came to be interpreted mystically as symbolizing either the hypostatic union or the union of Christ and the Church. Both understandings are included in the prayer "By the mystery of this water and wine," which is derived from an ancient Collect that addresses the mystery of the incarnation.

- The preparation of the chalice is a function of the deacon. When no deacon is present, the priest prepares the chalice. The one who prepares the chalice says the prayer "By the mystery of this water and wine" inaudibly.[165]

- The chalice may be prepared at the side table before the bread and wine are placed on the altar.[166]

---

165 See GIRM, no. 178.
166 See GIRM, no. 178.

Incense

108. Incense may be used at the Preparation of the Gifts as a sign of reverence for the elements and as acknowledgement of the presence and action of Christ in the priest celebrant and concelebrants and the rest of the congregation.[167]

- The priest incenses the gifts and the altar. The deacon or other minister incenses the priest and the congregation.

- When the members of the congregation or liturgical ministers are incensed, they stand.

Washing of Hands

109. While originating with a former need for the priest to wash his hands after assembling and arranging the elements of bread and wine and incensing them, the washing of hands was also well known in early Christianity, as in Judaism, as a symbolic expression of the need for inner purity at the beginning of a religious action.

- For the sake of authenticity, this action needs to be performed with dignity and deliberation. An appreciable quantity of water is poured from a pitcher, and the hands are dried with a towel.

---

167   See GIRM, no. 178.

- The words from Psalm 51, like the preceding "With humble and contrite hearts," are an expression of the priest's personal preparation and are not said audibly.

Prayer Over the Offerings

110. The Prayer Over the Offerings concludes the Preparation of the Gifts and points forward to the Eucharistic Prayer.

- The priest invites the people to pray using the formulary "Pray brothers and sisters" as prescribed in the *Order of Mass*.

- The prayer may be sung or said; the congregation responds, "Amen."

EUCHARISTIC PRAYER

111. The Eucharistic Prayer, the center and summit of the entire celebration, summarizes what it means for the Church to celebrate the Eucharist. It is a memorial proclamation of praise and thanksgiving for God's work of creation and salvation, a proclamation in which the Body and Blood of Christ are made present by the power of the Holy Spirit and in which the people are joined to Christ in offering his sacrifice to the Father. The Eucharistic Prayer is addressed to the Father through Jesus Christ, by the priest celebrant in the name of all who are present. The faithful profess their faith and give their assent through

dialogue, acclamations, and the Amen.[168] Since the Eucharistic Prayer is the summit of the Mass, its solemn nature and importance are enhanced when it is sung.

112. The Eucharistic Prayer is proclaimed over the Church's gifts. In the rich and varied tradition of this prayer, the Church gives praise and thanks for God's holiness and justice and for all God's mighty deeds in creating and redeeming the human race, deeds that reached their climax in the incarnation, life, death, and resurrection of Jesus Christ. In the Eucharistic Prayer the Last Supper is recounted; the mystery of Christ's passion, saving death, resurrection, and ascension is recalled; the memorial sacrifice of his Body and Blood is offered to the Father; and the Holy Spirit is invoked to sanctify the gifts and transform those who partake of them into the body of Christ, uniting them with the whole Church of God, living and dead, into one communion of love, service, and praise to the glory of the Father.

113. The following Eucharistic Prayers are either provided in the *Roman Missal* or otherwise approved for use in the United States of America.

- Eucharistic Prayers I through IV are the principal prayers and are for use throughout the liturgical year.

---

168   See GIRM, no. 78.

- The Eucharistic Prayers for Masses of Reconciliation I and II express thanksgiving in the context of the reconciliation won by Christ. They are particularly appropriate for use during the season of Lent and may be used at other times when the mystery of reconciliation is reflected in the readings or other texts of the Mass or when this mystery is being particularly emphasized at a particular gathering of the faithful.[169]

- A Eucharistic Prayer for Masses with Children may be used at Masses for preadolescent children or in which they constitute the majority of the assembly. The purpose of these texts is enhancing the participation of children in this central prayer of the Mass and preparing them to take full part in Masses with adults.[170] The Eucharistic Prayers for children, with their variety of acclamations, will be most effective in engaging the children when sung. The prayers use different levels of language and are rich in catechetical themes that may be drawn upon when preparing children for the Eucharistic celebration and for reflecting with them afterward on, for example, the nature of the Eucharist as thanksgiving for creation and salvation, the role of the Spirit and the real presence of Christ in the Eucharist and the Church, and the concepts of sacrifice, sacrament, and meal.

---

169 See EPMC, nos. 1-2.
170 See EPMC, no. 1; see DMC, no. 52.

- The Eucharistic Prayer for Masses for Various Needs and Occasions may be used in various circumstances. Its proper prefaces and closely related intercessions make it particularly suited for use with the formularies of the Masses for Various Needs and Occasions, which do not have their own proper prefaces.[171]

114. The following elements may be recognized as characteristics of the Eucharistic Prayer. Not all appear with equal force in every Eucharistic Prayer.[172]

Dialogue

115. Since the celebration of Mass is a communal action, the dialogue between priest celebrant and the congregation is of special value. It is not only an external sign of communal celebration, but also the means of greater interchange between priest and people.[173] The dialogue establishes at the outset that the Eucharistic Prayer is prayed in the person of Christ the Lord, who is with the Church, and in the name of the gathered assembly and indeed of the whole Church in heaven and on earth. All are invited, in biblical terms, to lift up their hearts: that is, to raise and place in God's presence their entire being, thoughts, memories, emotions, and expectations, in grateful attention and anticipation.

---

171 See *Eucharistic Prayer for Masses for Various Needs and Occasions*, August 6, 1991, Introduction, no. 1.
172 See GIRM, no. 79.
173 See GIRM, no. 34.

- The voice, gestures, and stance—the entire demeanor—of the priest celebrant help to convey the importance and the urgency of this movement, lifting all present and stimulating them to gratitude and wonder. This may be most effectively achieved by singing.

- Before the dialogue, the priest may introduce the Eucharistic Prayer by suggesting, very briefly, particular motives for thanksgiving.[174]

Preface

116. The praise and thanksgiving from which the entire Eucharist takes its name is especially concentrated in the "preface," which proclaims the Church's thanks for the saving work of God. In the Eastern tradition, this is a fixed part of the Eucharistic Prayer, beginning the praise of God and the rehearsal of God's mighty deeds that continue throughout the prayer. In the Roman tradition, the preface has been a variable element, stressing one aspect of God's saving work according to the day, the feast, the season, or the occasion. Many such prefaces from ancient and more recent sources are provided for use with Eucharistic Prayers I, II, and III.[175]

---

174 See GIRM, no. 31.
175 See GIRM, no. 79a.

- The preface is not a preliminary to the Eucharistic Prayer but is, rather, its first part. It indicates a proclamation, a speaking out before God and the faithful, rather than a foreword or prelude. For this reason, it is most appropriately sung.

- In the Eucharistic Prayer, the whole assembly of the faithful joins itself to Christ in acknowledging the great things God has done and, in the person of the priest, offers the sacrifice. It is the responsibility of the priest, acting in the person of Christ, the head of the Church, to proclaim the prayer for the people, to engage their attention, and to elicit their involvement throughout.[176]

- Eucharistic Prayer II has a proper preface—based, like the rest of the prayer, on an ancient Roman model—but other prefaces may be substituted, especially those that similarly present the mystery of salvation.[177]

- Eucharistic Prayer IV is constructed on an Eastern model. Its preface is a fixed and integral part of the prayer, whose themes continue beyond the *Sanctus*. For this reason, it is always to be used with its own preface. This is also true of the Eucharistic Prayers in Particular Circumstances.

---

176   See GIRM, nos. 27, 78.
177   See GIRM, no. 365b.

Sanctus Acclamation

117. In the *Sanctus* acclamation (or "Holy, Holy"), those present join their voices to that of all creation in giving glory to God, with words inspired by the vision of Isaiah (Is 6:3). In each celebration of the Eucharist, the Church is taken up into the eternal liturgy in which the entire communion of saints, the heavenly powers, and all of creation give praise to the God of the universe.

This acclamation is an integral part of the Eucharistic Prayer. It belongs to priest and people together. By its very nature it is meant to be sung, even if the preface is not. Choir or cantor parts may also be sung if they facilitate and enhance the congregation's participation.[178]

Epiclesis

118. In the sections of the prayer before and after the narrative of the institution, the Church invokes God's Spirit to hallow the gifts offered by the hands of the priest and make them the Body and Blood of Christ, and to gather those who receive them into a true communion of faith and love. Through the sanctifying power of the Holy Spirit, the repetition of the Lord's words of institution is efficacious, the memorial of Christ's death and resurrection is brought about, and the Church is built up again as the body of Christ in the world.[179]

---

178 See GIRM, no. 79b.
179 See GIRM, no. 79c.

- The life-giving power of the Spirit, who moved over the waters in the first days of creation and overshadowed Mary in the moment of the incarnation, is vividly expressed by the ancient gesture of bringing together the hands with the palms downward and extended over the elements to be consecrated. Especially when done with the proper gravity and deliberation, this gesture can reinforce powerfully the understanding of the words of the Spirit's action. This laying-on of the hands is the same sacramental gesture used in Ordination, Confirmation, Anointing of the Sick, and the Sacrament of Reconciliation.

- In accord with ancient tradition, concelebrating priests stretch out both their hands toward the elements.[180]

- "A little before the consecration . . . a server rings a bell as a signal to the faithful." Depending on local custom, the server may also ring the bell at the showing of both the Eucharistic Bread and the chalice.[181]

Institution Narrative and Consecration

119. At the heart of the Eucharistic Prayer, the account of the Last Supper is recited. Everything for which God has been thanked and praised—all that was accomplished in the history of salvation—is summed up and made present in the person of

---

180   See GIRM, no. 222a.
181   See GIRM, no. 150.

the crucified and risen Lord. The words of Jesus, in which he gave himself to his disciples as their food and drink, are repeated in fidelity to his command that they carry on this mystery.[182] In the power of the Spirit, these words achieve what they promise and express: the presence of Christ and his sacrifice among his people assembled in his name.

- This narrative is an integral part of the one continuous prayer of thanksgiving and blessing. It should be proclaimed in a manner that does not separate it from its context of praise and thanksgiving.

- As a narrative, it is also recited for the benefit of all present. It should therefore be proclaimed most reverently, audibly, and intelligibly.

- On concluding the words over the host, the priest shows the Sacred Body of the Lord to the people, and he subsequently does the same with the chalice.

Memorial Acclamation

120. The Memorial Acclamation of the people in the Eucharistic Prayer confesses the Church's belief in the Paschal Mystery of Christ's death, resurrection, and presence among his people.

---

182   See GIRM, no. 79d.

The Memorial Acclamations provided are not specific to the Eucharistic Prayers; each may be used with any of the prayers. As acclamations they are intended to be sung.

Anamnesis and Offering

121. The whole action of the Eucharist is done in obedience to the Lord's command, as a memorial of him. The Church understands this memorial as a living re-presentation before God of the saving deeds that he has accomplished in Christ, so that their fullness and power may be effective here and now. In this memorial re-presentation, the Church offers the one sacrifice of praise and thanksgiving, a sacramental offering of the sacrifice made "once for all" by Christ, the "holy and living sacrifice" that "brings salvation to all the world." It is an offering made by the whole Church, but especially by those here and now assembled who, in the power of the Holy Spirit, are called upon to offer themselves with and through Christ, the Victim and Priest who joins the Church's offering to his.[183]

Intercessions

122. By the grace of the Holy Spirit, the Church has become a single offering in Christ to the glory of God the Father. She now prays that the fruits of this sacrifice may be experienced throughout the Church and the world. (In Eucharistic Prayer I, the intercessions are divided by the institution narrative.) The Blessed

---

183   See GIRM, nos. 79e, 21.

Virgin Mary and the saints are named as the prime examples of the fruits of this redemptive sacrifice and as forerunners in the communion of the living and the dead. Praying in communion with Mary and the other saints of God, the Church now intercedes for the living and the dead in union with the Lord, who forever lives to make intercession (see Heb 7:25).[184]

- The saints enumerated in Eucharistic Prayer I include— besides the outstanding figures of the apostolic Church—the great figures and martyrs of the local Church of Rome. The names enclosed in brackets may be omitted from Eucharistic Prayer I. On the other hand, a local patron or a saint whose solemnity, feast, or memorial is being celebrated, or whose name is inscribed in the *Martyrology* for the day, may be mentioned in the intercessions of Eucharistic Prayer III, even when such a full liturgical celebration is not possible due to its coincidence with a day of higher rank in the liturgical calendar.[185]

- The Bishop of the diocese is to be named without fail in the Eucharistic Prayer, as is the Bishop—or exceptionally, the priest—who is equivalent to him in law. Such a figures include (a) a Bishop still retaining administration of a diocese after being transferred to another; (b) a Prelate having jurisdiction over a territory not attached to any diocese;

---

184   See GIRM, no. 79f.
185   See GNLYC, no. 49.

(c) a vicar apostolic; (d) an apostolic administrator when he is a Bishop and is fully exercising his office; (e) a prefect apostolic; and (f) an Abbot having jurisdiction over a territory not attached to any diocese. The coadjutor and auxiliary Bishops and other Bishops living in the diocese may also be named, if desired—using a general formula if there are several.[186]

Doxology

123. Faithful to the custom of Jesus and his Apostles, the Eucharistic Prayer concludes where it begins: with an ascription of praise and glory to God that is endorsed and ratified by all present in their acclamation "Amen." St. Paul considered the ratification by the congregation to be essential to the prayers of thanksgiving (see 1 Cor 14:15-16); and early Christian Fathers, such as St. Justin Martyr, greatly stressed the congregation's "Amen" as the people's confirmation of all that has been proclaimed on their behalf by the priest.[187]

124. Through Christ, with him, and in him, all is turned to the Father's glory by the action of the Holy Spirit. At this climax of the prayer, the consecrated elements are raised in a gesture that vividly expresses the true nature of the Eucharistic sacrifice as the offering of the Church through Christ the High

---

186 See GIRM, no. 149; see Sacred Congregation for Divine Worship, decree *Cum de nomine* (*On Mention of the Bishop's Name in the Eucharistic Prayer*) (October 9, 1972): AAS 64 (1972).

187 See GIRM, no. 79h.

Priest; with Christ, who is really present in the Church; and in Christ, who has incorporated his people into himself by the action of the Holy Spirit.

- The profound importance of the congregation's ratification and acclamation can be difficult to bring out in the one short word "Amen." It should be at least sung or spoken vigorously both at the Sunday celebration and at simply weekday celebrations. Musical settings that prolong or repeat the "Amen" can help the congregation to experience and express its true power.

- At the conclusion of the Eucharistic Prayer, the priest should make a distinct pause to emphasize that the Eucharistic Prayer (the "giving thanks") is complete and that the communion rite (the "breaking and sharing") is about to begin.

COMMUNION RITE

125. The reception together of the Lord's Body and Blood in a paschal meal is the culmination of the Eucharist. Those present are made ready to share in this banquet by a rite that leads from the Eucharistic Prayer directly to the Communion. This rite expresses the mutual love and reconciliation that are both the condition and the fruit of worthy communion and the

unity of the many in the one symbolized at both the natural and the sacramental level.[188]

- Though each of these rites (the Lord's Prayer, sign of peace, breaking of the bread) is important in itself, in the context of the whole celebration they constitute together a transition from one high point, the Eucharistic Prayer, to another, the sharing in Holy Communion. Their musical treatment should not be so elaborate as to give the impression that they are of greater significance than the Eucharistic Prayer that precedes them or the reception of Holy Communion that follows them and is accompanied by communal song.

The Lord's Prayer

126. The community of the baptized is constituted as the family of God by the Spirit of adoption. In the fullness of this Spirit, who has once again been invoked upon them, they call upon him as Father. Because of its themes of daily bread and mutual forgiveness, the Lord's Prayer has been used in all liturgical traditions as a most appropriate preparation for Holy Communion, "so that what is holy may, in fact, be given to those who are holy."[189] The final petition is expanded into a prayer that concludes with the congregational doxology or acclamation "For the kingdom," which was appended to the Lord's Prayer in some of the earliest liturgical texts and in texts of the New Testament.

---

188   See GIRM, no. 80.
189   GIRM, no. 81.

- As the family prayer of all God's children, the Lord's Prayer belongs to all the baptized. When sung, it is sung by everyone together. In this case, it will normally be desirable for the priest to sing the embolism ("Deliver us, Lord . . .") that follows and for the priest and people together to sing the concluding acclamation "For the kingdom."

Sign of Peace

127. A sign of peace, which in earlier times took the form of a ritual kiss, is mentioned in the oldest writings of the New Testament and is found in the Eucharistic liturgy from the earliest days of the Church (see Rom 16:16). In the Roman liturgical tradition, it found its place after the Lord's Prayer, whose themes of mutual forgiveness it echoes, and it thus has an important connection with the reception of Holy Communion. In the early Church, it was described as a "seal" placed on prayer.

128. The biblical concept of peace includes total well-being, a life in harmony with God and with ourselves, with our neighbors, and with the whole of creation. Such peace can only be the pure gift of God. It is won for us by the risen Christ present in the midst of those gathered, and so it is the peace of Christ that is exchanged.

129. The exchange of peace before the reception of Holy Communion acknowledges that Christ whom we receive in the sacrament is already present in our neighbor. In this exchange,

all present acknowledge the insistent Gospel truth that communion with God in Christ is enjoyed in communion with our brothers and sisters in Christ. The rite of peace is not an expression merely of human solidarity or good will; it is, rather, an opening of ourselves and our neighbors to a challenge and a gift from beyond ourselves. Like the "Amen" at Communion, the exchange of peace is the acceptance of a challenge: a gesture expressing the belief that we are members, one with another, in the body of Christ.

- The priest may give the sign of peace to the ministers, but he always remains within the sanctuary, so as not to disturb the celebration. In the dioceses of the United States of America, with good reason on special occasions (for example, at a funeral or wedding, or when civic leaders are present), the priest may offer the sign of peace to a few faithful near the sanctuary. All exchange the sign of peace with those nearest to them. The greeting "May the peace of the Lord be always with you" may be used, with the response "Amen."[190]

- The sign itself is sufficiently strong and expressive and does not need explanatory song or commentary. Thus, no song or commentary should accompany the exchange of the sign of peace.

---

190   See GIRM, no. 154.

Breaking of the Bread

130. This characteristic action of Christ at the feeding of the multitude, at the Last Supper, and at his meals with the disciples after his resurrection in the days of the Apostles gave its name to the entire celebration of the Eucharist. The natural, the practical, the symbolic, and the spiritual are all inextricably linked in this most powerful symbol. Just as many grains of wheat are ground, kneaded, and baked together to become one loaf, which is then broken and shared out among many to bring them into one table-fellowship, so those gathered are made one body in the one bread of life that is Christ (see 1 Cor 10:17).

131. In order for the meaning of this symbolism to be perceived, both the bread and the breaking must be truly authentic and recognizable. The Eucharistic bread is to "have the appearance of food" and is to be made so that it can be broken and distributed to at least some of the members of the congregation.[191]

- The faithful are not ordinarily to be given Holy Communion from the tabernacle with hosts consecrated at a previous Mass.[192] When, for genuine pastoral reasons—for example, the late arrival of unexpected numbers—the hosts consecrated at the Mass must be supplemented with reserved consecrated hosts from the tabernacle, these hosts may be

---

191 See GIRM, no. 321.
192 See SC, no. 55; see EuchMyst, nos. 31-32; see GIRM, no. 123.

brought reverently but without ceremony from the tabernacle to the altar at the breaking of the bread.

- The bread is broken with dignity and deliberation, normally by the priest celebrant, who may be assisted by the deacon or a concelebrant. It begins after the exchange of peace is finished and when the attention of the faithful is again focused on the action taking place at the holy table.

- The regular use of larger breads will foster an awareness of the fundamental symbolism in which all, priest and people, share in the same host. At every Mass, at least one large host is broken into several portions. One of these portions is consumed by the priest, while the rest are distributed to at least a few others.

- During the breaking of the bread, the *Agnus Dei* ("Lamb of God") is sung or said. All call on Christ Jesus as the Lamb of God (see Jn 1:29, 36) who has conquered sin and death (see 1 Pt 1:18 and Rev 5:6, 13:8). The *Agnus Dei* is a litany intended to accompany the action of breaking and may therefore be prolonged by repetition until such time as the action is completed.

- If additional Sacred Vessels are needed for the distribution of Holy Communion, they may be brought to the altar at this point. The consecrated hosts are then reverently divided among the patens or ciboria by the priest or deacon, and the Precious Blood is poured into the chalices.

- If extraordinary ministers assist in the distribution of Holy Communion, they come to the altar after the communion of the priest.

Communion

PRIVATE PREPARATION OF THE PRIEST

132. The prayer for the private preparation of the priest is recited inaudibly. At this time, the faithful prepare themselves quietly for Holy Communion.[193]

INVITATION TO HOLY COMMUNION

133. The consecrated elements are raised up and shown to the people using the words that express the confidence of the baptized and to which they respond with the humility of the centurion (see Mt 8:9). The priest celebrant takes the host and elevates it above the paten or chalice in a gesture that is demonstrative and dignified.[194]

---

193   See GIRM, no. 84f.
194   See GIRM, no. 157.

DISTRIBUTION OF HOLY COMMUNION

134. Faithful to the Lord's command to his disciples to "take and eat" and "take and drink," the congregation completes the Eucharistic action by eating and drinking together the Body and Blood of Christ consecrated during the celebration. For this reason, the faithful should not ordinarily be given Holy Communion from the tabernacle. Also for this reason, for the faithful to share the chalice is most desirable, insofar as this is provided for by the norms of the Holy See, the diocesan Bishop, and the USCCB.[195] Drinking at the Eucharist is a sharing in the sign of the new covenant (see Lk 22:20), a foretaste of the heavenly banquet (see Mt 26:29), a sign of participation in the suffering Christ (see Mk 10:38-39).[196]

135. Although a communion procession is not obligatory and is not always possible, it should be the normal arrangement for both practical and symbolic reasons. It expresses the humble patience of the poor moving forward to be fed, the alert expectancy of God's people sharing the paschal meal in readiness for their journey, the joyful confidence of God's people on the march toward the promised land. The dioceses of the United States of America are given four options for the communion song: (1) the antiphon and psalm from the *Roman Missal* as set to music in the *Roman Gradual* or another musical setting; (2) the seasonal antiphon

---

195   See GIRM, no. 283.
196   See GIRM, nos. 72c, 83, 281, 282, 283.

and psalm of the *Simple Gradual*; (3) a song from another collection of psalms and antiphons, approved by the USCCB or the diocesan Bishop, including psalms arranged in responsorial or metrical forms; or (4) a suitable liturgical song chosen in accord with GIRM, no. 86.

136. A sufficient number of ministers should assist in the distribution of Holy Communion.

- In all that pertains to Communion under both kinds, *Norms for the Distribution and Reception of Holy Communion Under Both Kinds in the Dioceses of the United States of America* is to be followed.[197] When Holy Communion is administered under both kinds, the deacon who ministers the chalice is to receive Holy Communion from the priest under both kinds and then administer the chalice to the faithful; after the distribution of Holy Communion, he then reverently consumes any of the Precious Blood left in the chalice, being assisted, if necessary, by other deacons and priests.[198] If many priests are concelebrating, the Communion of the congregation need not be delayed but may begin after the presiding celebrant has communicated.

---

197   See GIRM, no. 283; see also United States Conference of Catholic Bishops, *Norms for the Distribution and Reception of Holy Communion Under Both Kinds in the Dioceses of the United States of America*, Liturgy Documentary Series 13 (Washington, D.C.: United States Conference of Catholic Bishops, 2002).
198   See GIRM, no. 182.

There is no need for all the concelebrating priests to finish receiving Holy Communion before distribution to the congregation can commence, as long as the concelebrants are able to continue receiving Communion while it is also being distributed to the faithful.[199]

- Extraordinary ministers of Holy Communion are not permitted to receive Holy Communion after the manner of the concelebrants (i.e., to self-communicate); instead they are to be given Holy Communion by one of the ordinary ministers of the sacrament.[200]

- In the United States of America, Holy Communion may be received in the hand as well as on the tongue; the choice is the prerogative of the communicant. The faithful are not permitted to take up the consecrated bread or the sacred chalice themselves and still less to hand them to one another.

- Children, like adults, have the option to receive Holy Communion in the hand or on the tongue. No limitations because of age have been established. Careful preparation for first reception of the Eucharist will provide the necessary instruction.[201]

---

199   See GCE, no. 47.

200   *Interdicasterial Instruction on Certain Questions Regarding the Collaboration of the Non-Ordained Faithful in the Sacred Ministry of Priests* (*Ecclesiae de mysterio*) (Washington, D.C.: United States Conference of Catholic Bishops, 1998), art. 8.

201   See *Holy Communion Outside Mass* (Washington, D.C.: United States Conference of Catholic Bishops, 1983), no. 21.

- When receiving the Eucharist in the hand, the communicant approaches the minister with one hand resting on the palm of the other. After responding, "Amen," the communicant steps to the side and reverently places the Eucharist in his or her mouth.

- When Holy Communion is distributed under both kinds by intinction, the Eucharist is not placed in the hands of the communicants, nor may the communicants receive the Eucharist and then dip it into the chalice themselves. In distributing Holy Communion by intinction, the minister says, "The Body and Blood of Christ," and the communicant responds, "Amen." Intinction should not be introduced as a means of circumventing the practice of taking Communion in the hand.

- When the USCCB and the diocesan Bishop have determined, in conformity with the norms set forth by the Holy See, that Communion under both kinds may be given, the pastor or priest celebrant should see to its full and proper implementation. Even when Communion is given under both kinds, however, the communicant may choose not to drink from the chalice.[202]

202　See GIRM, no. 284.

- The norm for the posture of reception of Holy Communion in the dioceses of the United States is standing. However, communicants who kneel should not be denied Holy Communion because they kneel. Rather, such instances should be addressed pastorally, by providing the faithful with proper catechesis on the reasons for this norm.

- When receiving Holy Communion standing, the communicant bows his or her head before the sacrament as a gesture of reverence and receives the Body of the Lord from the minister. When Holy Communion is received under both kinds, the sign of reverence is also made before receiving the Precious Blood.[203]

COMMUNION SONG

137. The Communion of priest and people is traditionally accompanied by the singing of a psalm with a simple congregational refrain. Any psalm or other hymn is appropriate if it expresses the spiritual unity of the communicants, shows the joy of all, and makes the communion procession an act of union of brothers and sisters in Christ. In its structure and its simplicity, the song should encourage the participation of all present.[204]

- The communion song begins while the priest is receiving Holy Communion.[205]

---

203   See EuchMyst, no. 34a; see GIRM, no. 160.
204   See GIRM, no. 87.
205   See GIRM, no. 86.

- So as not to encumber the congregation with books or scripts during the procession, the singing may be led by cantor or choir and include a repeated response from the congregation.

- Although several communion songs may be sung in succession, depending on the length of Communion, it may be preferable to interrupt congregational singing with periods of silence, instrumental music (in seasons when it is not excluded), or choral music, resuming the singing after an interlude.

- Some traditional Eucharistic hymns that were composed for Benediction of the Most Blessed Sacrament—and therefore concentrate on adoration rather than on the action of Communion—may not be appropriate as communion songs.

PURIFICATION OF SACRED VESSELS

138. When the distribution of Holy Communion is completed, the altar is cleared and the Sacred Vessels are purified.

- Although performed with reverence, the purification should be done briefly and inconspicuously; especially if several Sacred Vessels must be purified, they may be covered, placed on a corporal at a side table, and purified as soon as possible after Mass.

- This purification—by a priest, deacon, or instituted acolyte—is carried out, if possible, at the side table. However, if necessary it may be done at the altar—and, if so, at the side of the altar rather than at the center.[206]

- Pouring the Precious Blood into the ground or into the sacrarium is strictly prohibited.[207]

PERIOD OF SILENCE OR SONG OF PRAISE

139. After the distribution of Holy Communion, all may observe a period of silence. The absence of all words, actions, music, or movement offers an opportunity for interior prayer and contemplation on the Eucharistic mystery. Such silence is important to the rhythm of the whole celebration and is welcome in a busy and restless world.

- Silence and true stillness can be achieved if all take part—congregation and liturgical ministers alike.

- This period of deep and tranquil communion is not to be interrupted by the taking of a second collection or by parish announcements, which (if needed) come correctly in the concluding rite. Nor should this silence be broken or overlaid by the public reading or recitation of devotional material.

---

206   See GIRM, nos. 163, 279.
207   See CIC, c. 1367; see also *Norms for the Distribution and Reception of Holy Communion Under Both Kinds in the Dioceses of the United States of America*, no. 55.

- As an alternative or addition to silent contemplation, a psalm or other song of praise may be sung.[208]

Prayer After Communion

140. In a final presidential prayer that brings to a close the communion rite, the priest prays for the community of faith, asking that the spiritual effects of the Eucharist be experienced in the lives of the faithful.[209] The prayer may be sung or said; the congregation responds, "Amen."

---

208   See GIRM, nos. 88, 164
209   See GIRM, no. 89.

V.

CONCLUDING RITE

141. After the communion rite, the Mass closes with a brief concluding rite. Its purpose is to send the people forth to put into effect in their daily lives the Paschal Mystery and unity in Christ that they have celebrated. They are given a sense of abiding mission that calls them to witness to Christ in the world and to bring the Gospel to the poor.

142. The concluding rite consists of the priest celebrant's greeting and blessing, which on certain days and occasions is expanded by the prayer over the people or other solemn blessings. This is followed by the dismissal and an orderly procession of the ministers. The whole rite may be preceded by necessary but brief pastoral announcements.[210]

When another liturgical rite is to follow immediately—for example, the final commendation at a funeral—the entire concluding rite is omitted because these other rites have their own form of conclusion.[211]

Announcements

143. Just as the introductory comments by the priest at the beginning of the celebration may help those present to better

---

210   See GIRM, nos. 166, 168.
211   See GIRM, no. 170.

appreciate and experience the mysteries celebrated in the Eucharist, so also may the pastoral announcements at the end help the people make the transition from worship into renewed Christian witness in society. They should help people become aware of the faith life and pastoral activity of the community and invite participation in the ongoing work of the Church.

- Ordinarily, announcements, when required, should be brief enough for the congregation to remain standing.

- In order to respect the dignity of the ambo as the place of God's word, announcements are made from some other place.

- Announcements may be made by the deacon, by the priest if he prefers, or by another member of the community chosen for this purpose.[212]

Greeting

144. The greeting "The Lord be with you" helps the congregation again to focus attention on the prayerful aspect of blessing.

Blessing

145. As Scripture attests, all beings are created and kept in existence by God's gracious goodness. They are themselves

---

212   See GIRM, no. 184.

blessings from God and should move us to bless God in return. This is above all true since the Word has come in flesh to make all things holy by the mystery of the incarnation.

146. Blessings, therefore, refer first and foremost to God, whose majesty and goodness they extol, and they involve human beings, whom God governs and by divine providence protects.[213]

- The priest celebrant is encouraged to give a more solemn form of blessing on Sundays and holy days. He may use either a solemn blessing or a prayer over the people. When either of these forms of blessing is used, it is the function of the deacon, after the greeting, to invite the people to dispose themselves in reverence to receive the blessing.

- In the case of the solemn blessing, the priest extends his hands over the people as he sings or says the formula of the blessing in such a way that the congregation is clearly invited to respond with an "Amen" to each invocation. The threefold solemn blessings touch upon various aspects of a feast or of divine graciousness, and often they affirm the mission of the lay faithful in the world.

- In the case of a prayer over the people, which by contrast is simpler and more general in content, the priest uses the same gesture of extending his hands over the people.

---

213 See *Book of Blessings* (1987), General Introduction, no. 7.

- When a Bishop presides, in addition to these formularies he may use other special formularies of blessing reserved to him.

- These various forms of blessing conclude always with the Trinitarian formulary, during which the priest with his right hand traces the Sign of the Cross over the congregation as they make the Sign of the Cross on themselves.

Dismissal

147. The dismissal sends the members of the congregation forth to praise and bless the Lord in the midst of their daily responsibilities.[214]

- The deacon says or sings the dismissal, using one of the prescribed formularies.[215]

- The response "Thanks be to God" is a statement of grateful praise for encountering the risen Christ in the Church's worship.

- Beginning at the Easter Vigil and continuing up to and including the Second Sunday of Easter, the double "Alleluia" is added to the dismissal and the response. It is also added on Pentecost.

---

214 See GIRM, no. 90.
215 See GIRM, no. 185.

- The prescribed words of dismissal reflect the sacredness of the ritual. Casual remarks or secular forms of farewell are out of place, as they distract from the dignity of the rite.

- The priest celebrant and deacon kiss the altar.[216]

- All ministers then make a profound bow to the altar; or, if the tabernacle in which the Blessed Sacrament is reserved is present, they genuflect to it.[217] They then leave in the same order in which they entered at the beginning of the celebration.[218]

- If they have not left earlier, extraordinary ministers who are to bring Holy Communion to the sick may take their place in the procession.

- The procession may be accompanied by a song of praise, seasonal hymn, appropriate instrumental music, or even, on some occasions, silence. A recessional song is always optional, even for solemn occasions.

---

216   See GIRM, nos. 169, 186.
217   See GIRM, no. 274.
218   See GIRM, no. 169.